Mary Sandreth   Nov. 11, 1995

GUIDE ME
— TO —
Eternity

CHRISTINE TUTTLE MONSEN
WITH STAN ZENK

ASPEN BOOKS

Salt Lake City, Utah

Guide Me to Eternity
Copyright 1994 by Christine Tuttle Monsen

Library of Congress Cataloging-in-Publication Data

Monsen, Christine
    Guide me to eternity / by Christine Monsen with Stan Zenk.
         p. cm.
    ISBN 1-56236-215-1 : $11.95
    1. Monsen, Christine. 2. Mormon women—United States—Biography.
3. Death—Religious aspects—Mormon Church. 4. Death—Religious aspects—Church of Jesus Christ of Latter-Day Saints. 5. Bereavement—Religious aspects—Mormon Church. 6. Bereavement—Religious aspects—Church of Jesus Christ of Latter-Day Saints.
    I. Zenk, Stan. II. Title.
    BX8695.M55A3 1994
    248.8'6—dc20   94-24151
                                                CIP

10   9   8   7   6   5   4   3   2

Cover Design: Susan Lofgren
Photo enhancing: Neil Brown
Cover photography: Matthew Reier
Author photos: John Luke

"Fathers," pg. 132, words by Dawn Hughes Ballantyne. ©The Church of Jesus Christ of Latter-day Saints. Used by permission.

Dedication

To my husband, John Monsen, for giving me everlasting happiness. John's loving guidance gives me assurance that we will be together forever. I thank him for his love of life, which has given me six wonderful children: Melanie, Stephanie, Jennifer, Michael John, Clinton Lewis, and John Jared. I thank him for these gifts, for through our children I find continuous joy and happiness.

Acknowledgments

To my family for your continuing desire to give me strength. To each of you, my mother and father, Bill and Charlene Tuttle; my sisters and their spouses, Jill and Les Birch, Jayne and Rob Taylor, Tracie and Jim Larsen, Laurie and David Lund; and my brothers and their spouses, Ken and Lori Tuttle, Kelly and Denise Tuttle. I am so blessed to have each one of you and your families in my life. You have truly been there to help me and my children in our time of need. To my loving parents for teaching me the meaning of hard work and the desire to excel in my life. You have taught me well. Thank you.

To John's family who played such an important part in his life. John's mother and father, Lewis and Janet Monsen, for raising a wonderful son and teaching him strong family values. To his sisters and their spouses, Julie and Lynn Syddall, Madalyn and Rick Bennett, and his brothers and their spouses, Robert and Teresa Monsen, Bryce and Sharlene Monsen, Gary and Maylene Monsen, for always helping each other and staying a close family. I thank you all for many acts of kindness and love.

To my children. Thank you, Melanie, Stephanie, and Jennifer for taking such good care of your brothers, Michael, Clint, and John. I thank my Heavenly Father every day for the wonderful children he has blessed me with. You are my life and you bring me joy and happiness. Thank you for your love, your hugs, and your constant giving one to another so I could have the time to work on this book. I know that the one most important thing we can take with us into the eternities is the love we feel for each other.

I feel sincere gratitude for the loving people of Holden, Utah. Many, many times you have built us up and given my children and me much love and concern. You are wonderful people and I am so grateful I was living in Holden when John died. Your love has helped me endure and helped me face the tragedy of losing my husband.

To my dearest friend, Lorna Stevens, whose everlasting friendship has been my encouragement. You instilled in my heart the importance of writing this book. A special thanks to her husband, Roger, who has been patient and understanding through Lorna's many hours of service.

To Jason North for helping me edit the first draft of my manuscript. Your help, time, and talents were sincerely appreciated.

To the diligent and caring staff at Aspen Books for their second-mile efforts—especially Darla Isackson, whose leadership and love for this book pulled it through the production process.

To Stan Zenk for his insight, many hours of hard work and dedication. I feel you are an answer to many hours of prayer. You have been the tool in making this book possible. Your writing skills coupled with your continuing inspiration and faith have made it possible for this book's message to be the way our brother and Savior Jesus Christ wanted it to be. I will always be eternally grateful for what you have accomplished.

Chris and John Monsen with children (left to right): Stephanie,
Clint, Michael, Little Johnny, Jennifer, and Melanie

GUIDE ME
— TO —
Eternity

Chapter One

Sometimes I remember the calm of that Monday morning seven years ago and long to have it back. The house was quiet. We were lying asleep in our beds and unaware that on that day our lives would change forever. Sometimes I remember the innocence of that morning and, with all my heart, long for its return—his return.

Something pulled me from my sleep. I looked at the alarm clock, and suddenly it buzzed, sending a jolt of fear through my body like a danger signal. Fumbling for the knob, I switched it off. Light shone through the curtains. I reached for John lying beside me.

"You okay?" he asked.

"It was the alarm," I said, willing my heart to settle.

He laughed and I felt a little silly. That familiar queasy feeling made its way up from my stomach. It was morning sickness. I pulled the covers over my shoulders. "Wouldn't it be nice to sleep in?" I said.

Johnny rolled over and pulled me to him. "Sleep in?" he said, kissing me quickly on the lips. "My first day off in twelve *endless* days, and you want to sleep in? Chris, let's get up and do something fun. Take the kids somewhere. See some sights. Who wants to sleep in?"

I looked into his face, inches from mine. He was irresistible. Primed for adventure, his eyes were shining like a little kid's. Snap out of it! I wanted to say. I didn't feel good and I wanted to stay home. But he had worked two six-day shifts without a break. Now he had four days off and he was determined to take them at full advantage. During his twenty-nine years, John had seldom done anything half-heartedly. Approaching each day with enthusiasm, he worked and played with equal vigor. For eight years I had been his companion. I had borne him five children, and in eight more months, we were expecting a sixth. During our years together, I had entwined my life with his and had been the full-time beneficiary of his love for life. John was the mortal light and life of my own soul.

But sometimes he made me tired.

I pushed my fingers into his sandy-red hair and felt the warmth of his head in my palm. I resisted the urge to make a fist and yank. Staring irrepressibly out of those hazel eyes was that boy, and I knew there would be no keeping him home today.

"Okay." I gave in. "Tell you what. You stay here and think about what you want to do and I'll get out of bed long enough to get Melanie and Stephanie off to school. Then we'll talk."

"Deal." He smiled and lay back against the pillows.

I was suddenly reluctant to leave the warmth of the covers and the solid comfort of my husband. A feeling came over me that all was not well. Besides feeling sick to my stomach, something else nagged at me, and I thought: If anything happens today... But I put the feeling aside, swung my legs out, and slowly stood up. It was a quiet April morning. The air was cool on my arms and legs.

I roused our two oldest and told them to get ready for school. Jennifer, four; Michael, three; and Clint, eighteen-months, could sleep a little longer.

I shuffled into the kitchen and opened the fridge to start breakfast. The smell of yesterday's onions and tuna fish assaulted me and my stomach did a barrel roll. I was going to be sick. I slammed the fridge and ran for the bathroom.

Seven-year-old Melanie, our oldest, was at the door. "Mommy, are you okay?"

"No, honey, but I'll feel better in a minute. Could you get the cereal down and pour the milk for Stephanie?"

"Okay. Mommy, is the smell of food getting to you again?"

"Yes," I said.

"Is what you've got catching?" she asked. "I hope I don't get it."

I sat down on the edge of the tub and laughed weakly. "Melanie, one thing you don't have to worry about is catching my sickness." We hadn't told the kids yet about the pregnancy. I was only five weeks along.

After the girls finished eating I felt better and called them in to do their hair. Stephanie, our preschooler, wanted to know if I had the flu. I assured her I was all right and started in on her ponytail. When the girls were done I told them to brush their teeth and go to the living room for family prayer. Fresh and smiling in new spring outfits, they ran out and hugged their dad. John enveloped them in his strong arms. "I love you, Daddy," they said in turn. "I love you, too," he answered.

The morning sun sent a river of light through the windows. We knelt in its glow, and John's voice was warm in prayer. It enfolded us, soothed our spirits, transported us heavenward. His words that morning were the most beautiful I had heard him say. I wish I could remember them. They formed the last prayer I ever heard my husband offer.

When the prayer ended, we stood and bustled the girls out for the bus. Johnny said, "If we're not here when you get home from school, walk to Grandma Monsen's, okay guys?"

They said they would.

"And you know what? In a couple of days we'll go camping. What do you say?"

They were thrilled. The kids loved camping with their father. He was the consummate outdoorsman. Camping, hunting, horseback riding, boating—his enthusiasm for adventure was endless. He got such a kick from the outdoors that to be with him was a joy.

With thoughts of a camping trip quickening their steps, the two girls scurried off to catch the bus.

My own heart lighter, I returned to our bedroom, jumped quickly into bed, and squirmed down under the covers. John came in. "Hey, Chris. What are you doing?"

He sounded a little impatient. When there were things to be done, John liked to get on with them.

"Didn't we make a deal?" I said. "That I'd get the girls off and then get back in bed to make plans for the day?"

"Oh, right." He jumped in beside me. "I know. Let's go to Yuba Lake and waterski."

Well, that was quick, I thought, and realized he'd probably had it planned all along. I felt like resisting. "Waterski? You're crazy! It's April. The water will be freezing."

"Maybe, maybe not. These last two weeks have been like summer. I bet it's not that bad."

"John, we can't waterski today. I'm going to the doctor for my first visit. I hoped to get a shot for this morning sickness."

"But you'll feel better later on, won't you?"

It was true. I usually felt better around ten.

"You can see the doctor tomorrow," he continued, "and then you'll feel great for the rest of our vacation."

"But we talked about going to the temple tomorrow."

"We'll see the doctor first thing. There will be plenty of time for the trip to the temple. Sound okay? Today, Yuba Lake. Tomorrow, the doctor and the temple. And then Wednesday and Thursday we'll go camping. What do you say?"

I wanted to say I'm tired and I don't feel good and I want to stay home, but the words that came out of my mouth were, "Sounds great." It would be unfair to spoil his plans—he'd been working so hard. Emotion welled up inside me and I turned to him. "I love you," I said.

"I love you, too. You're not too sick to get ready?"

"No," I answered, though I felt an odd sadness.

He brightened. "Hey, Chris, we're going to have fun. You'll see."

"You know how I feel about Yuba Lake. I hate that place."

"Not that again, Chris."

"I just don't want anything to happen."

"Nothing will happen. It'll be okay."

He was used to reassuring me. The feeling that something was going to happen to John had come to me often over the years. Whenever he left on a trip or went off hunting with his dad and brothers, or sometimes when he simply left for work, a feeling would come to me that I might not see him again. I was especially nervous when he flew.

Besides his work as an electrician at IPP—the Intermountain Power Project—John was also a licensed pilot. He learned to fly from a man he idolized—Pete Shields, the owner of Delta Aviation. Often, when officials needed to fly in or out of Delta, Pete would hire John to pilot the plane. Sometimes I went along. And I was so convinced that something, sometime, would happen to John, that I talked Pete into giving me lessons on emergency landings so that if anything happened in the air, I would be able to land the plane. Johnny knew about my fears—we occasionally discussed them. He understood and did what he could to calm me whenever they arose.

These fears were not unfounded. They stemmed from something I learned the day we were married in the Manti Temple. The Spirit was strong that day *and* constant. John had picked me up early so we could drive from Holden together. It was a beautiful spring morning and we spoke of our love and happiness and of the sacred events that would take place later that morning. As we approached Manti, the sun rose in its brilliance from behind the mountain. When I saw the light hit the temple spires an impression came that John, this man at my side, was an elect son of God and that I was incredibly blessed to have him. That feeling stayed with me throughout the morning. The ceremony itself was beautiful. I was so very much in love and I knew without a doubt that we were following God's will, that our union was meant to be, and that something wonderful would come of it. I knew we would be husband and wife forever. And then, as the sealing ended and we stood to exchange rings, I was given to know, there by the altar in that holy place, that I must take good care of my new husband. That I must watch over him and love him, for I would not have him long.

And so I had lived, ever since, with this burden—knowing I'd lose him, but never knowing how or when. That morning, the first of John's vacation, I didn't know it would be that day, and so I did what I had always done before—I tried to put the feelings aside and not let them spoil our plans. John had said things would be okay. I smiled and responded, "If you say so." Then I got up, rubbed my arms to get some energy flowing, and added, "Just don't make me face that fridge again. I'd rather stop and *buy* food for the picnic than spend a minute in that kitchen." When you have morning sickness, food is best under cellophane.

"Sounds good," he said. "We'll stop at the store on the way."

Johnny jumped out of bed and went to the window. "What a beautiful day," he said.

I watched him pull on a pair of cutoffs over his swimming trunks and then put on a shirt.

He said, "While you get the kids up and going, I'll run to Mom and Dad's and get the boat ready. It shouldn't take long."

"John, I haven't seen you this excited since the day we were married." He had unabashedly *glowed* that whole day.

"I *am* excited. I haven't used those water skis for six months!"

"Oh. Well, I hope *I* was as good an acquisition as *they* were."

"Of course," he said. And a moment later, "Chris, do you think we will have another girl?" He sounded almost disappointed. Before our three girls were born, Johnny had been sure they would be boys. He had played football in high school for the Millard Eagles, and they had taken state in their division year after year, under the inspired direction of their coach, Johnny's dad. Sports were important in the family and important to John, and he wanted sons to share in them. He was the oldest of four boys, and he wanted to be the one to present the first grandson to the family. It had been a close race. A month before his brother's baby was due, our Michael was born. Though Johnny had loved his girls completely from the moment of their births, his joy was finally full with the birth of a son. And because he wanted Michael to grow up with girls *and* boys, he was thrilled again when Clint came along.

"You have *two* boys," I said. "Isn't that enough?"

"I would like another boy. Then it will be even. Three girls and three boys." As if they would be taking sides against each other.

I smiled. "I think I'll plan on another girl, and then if it's a boy, we'll be surprised."

"Well, my order is for a boy!" he said. A wide grin filled his face.

I followed him to the door and watched him head off in a run along the path leading to his parents' home. He was luminous in the morning light. John was strong and athletic. His body was firm, his movements graceful. I watched him run across the field and it seemed as though his feet didn't touch the ground.

Chapter Two

When John returned with the boat I was almost ready. Jennifer and the boys were in their swimsuits and I had grabbed the water jug and other things we would need. Excited for the trip, the kids were finding toys to play with in the sand. Yuba was one of their favorite spots. They loved riding in the boat. It was a Beachcraft Sea Swirl, that John had made faster by rebuilding the engine. He loved to throttle it wide and race the boat across the water. Yuba is bigger than nearby lakes, nearly fourteen miles long; enough open water to give the boat its full range. John liked it for that. Speed enraptured him. It tended to give me a bad case of M.E.A.S.—Mother's Extreme Anxiety Syndrome. I would fuss with the kids, making sure every last one had been strapped inextricably into a life jacket and aptly warned that they had better stay seated while the boat was in motion or I would personally clove hitch them to a docking moor. Actually, I didn't make a big enough deal out of it to ruin anyone's fun, but every time we roared away from the ramps I said a prayer in my heart, asking for a blessing—please Lord—of safety, this time out.

"That was quick," I said when Johnny burst in. I knew he had readied the boat and trailer, come home for our truck, driven it back to his parents' to hitch up the boat, and then returned home. That was too quick, I thought. "You haven't forgotten anything?"

"Nope. Everything's set." I could see he was anxious to get going.

"We're off then," I said and called for Jennifer, Michael, and Clint to get into the truck.

We loaded our gear into the boat and, after stopping for food and gas, headed north on the interstate. The drive was beautiful. The hills were green from recent spring rains. The smell of cedar and sage was invigorating. And John was in top form, laughing with the kids and talking about the fun we would have.

"I bet Melanie and Stephanie wish they were here," said Jennifer.

"I bet they do too, sweetie," I said. "It would be fun if we were all together."

I missed our two oldest daughters. John's work schedule of six days on and two days off did not coincide with school days and so we had gotten used to going on day outings without the older girls and then making it up by taking an extra trip later on. I thought of them in school and hoped they would be all right until we got home. They would at least be happy after school at Grandpa and Grandma Monsen's. Yuba Lake was only a half hour from home.

Somewhere north of the Scipio turnoff, Michael
asked, "Dad, are we going to catch a big one today?"

"No, son, not today. We're not going fishing, we're
going *boating*. You can play in the sand and we'll have a
picnic and lots of fun in the boat."

The fresh air had settled my stomach. Our plans were
sounding better and better. This may turn out to be a fun
day after all, I thought. I was glad to be doing what John
wanted on his day off, and I decided that, regardless of the
feelings I had earlier, I would help him enjoy it. I looked at
his beaming face and knew he was truly happy. To be out
with his family sporting around on a lovely day was
Johnny's favorite thing. And the closer we got to the lake,
the more the kids reflected his enthusiasm. We were all
feeling pretty excited and the warmth of my love for John
and my family welled up inside of me.

I grew up in Springville, Utah, and family values had
been a big part of my upbringing. To have a strong, gospel-
centered family, like John and I now enjoyed, had been my
goal all through my youth. When I became old enough, I
dated only boys who were members of the Church. That
was easy in Springville, but it became even easier when,
the summer before my senior year, we moved to Holden, a
smaller community which was almost completely LDS.
That's where I met Johnny.

It was at a youth activity and we had divided up into
teams to play football. He was on the other team and we
beat them, partly due to my speed running the ball. I had
run track in high school, and Johnny was impressed by my
ability. After the game he asked if he could walk me home.

I looked at him and saw this freckly-faced, redheaded kid, and I wasn't that interested. Strength in the gospel was important to me in a young man, but so were good looks. I didn't give him a chance.

A few weeks later at his mission farewell I wasn't any more favorably impressed. But when he came home from his mission, it was a different story. In the meantime I had graduated from high school and was attending BYU. It seemed to me that most young men there wanted to date me only because I danced with the Cougarettes. I saw a lack of sincerity in them that disappointed me. I was pleased, then, to listen to Johnny's homecoming talk and see his open-heartedness and his warmth. I was touched. And so was my father, who leaned across and said, "He's a nice guy, Chris. You should grab him while you can." And so I sat there in church, becoming more and more attracted to this now-handsome returned missionary. After the meeting when he asked me to his home for dinner, I accepted.

Two months later, before I left to travel with the Cougars to the 1978 Holiday Bowl in San Diego, John asked me to marry him and I said yes. We were married April 20, 1979—eight years to the week before our trip to Yuba Lake.

In those years together we had created my dream of a strong, gospel-centered family. We taught our children our deepest beliefs, and we served faithfully in our ward callings—me in Young Women and John in the elders quorum presidency. He was an example to me of dedication to church and family, which included our extended family. Both sets of parents lived nearby, and we had often taken trips like this one with them.

John turned the truck off the interstate and on to the state park road. Suddenly, the feeling returned that something was wrong and I became uneasy. I tried to push it aside and focus on the festivities ahead, but it lingered at the back of my mind. Was it a premonition, a warning, or was it just my dislike of Yuba Lake?

John had always liked Yuba. Situated between Levan and Scipio, it had been a favorite hangout for him and his high school buddies. He had many fond memories of the place. But I had never liked it, especially for family outings. It was too windy there. The water was cold and murky, and there weren't many beaches for the kids to play on. Also there was a dangerous drop-off not too far out in the water.

Once, when Jennifer was barely three, she had almost drowned at Yuba. She had gone out too far and started bobbing up and down trying to touch the bottom. Her life jacket came loose, and she slipped out through the bottom of it. I saw her go under and with a scream ran to help her. I was pregnant with Clint, so moving quickly was difficult, and being fully dressed made me even heavier in the water. I sloshed out to her and by the time I pulled her out, I was soaked to my neck in chilling water.

I had gotten angry—as parents do when their children have been in a dangerous situation—and I yelled at Johnny that I hated Yuba Lake and never ever wanted to come here again.

But John had thought my fears of the lake were unfounded. "It could've happened anywhere," he had said.

I disagreed. Delta Reservoir was a much safer place for the kids. It had wide sandy beaches and the water was shallow a long way out. The lake was not as deep as Yuba and so the water was not as cold. Sheltered from the wind, its waters were less rough and murky. But Delta Reservoir was smaller and was not as ideal for waterskiing. So John had chosen Yuba Lake this time. I only hoped we were early enough to beat the winds which usually increased as the day wore on.

My husband's voice pulled me from my brooding. "We're almost there. Who's going to see it first?"

Jennifer did. "Daddy, I see it!" she yelled, bouncing in her seat.

The lake swung into view, milky sapphire against the brown and green hills encircling it. It was a splendid sight. Light from the mid-morning sun glimmered on its surface beneath a boundless sky.

However, as the truck approached the lake, we could see that the wind was already kicking up a few waves.

"The water looks choppy, John," I said. "What do you think?"

Though I could see the disappointment on his face, he was not going to let a little wind change his plans. "I think it'll be okay," he said. "This is a big lake. We're bound to find a place where the water is smooth. It's such a great day for skiing!"

He was so eager and his mind was made up. Though the uneasy feeling still haunted me, I didn't want to ruin John's first day of vacation, and so I said, "Okay, let's do it."

John drove into the state park and stopped near the station to pay the fee. His friend Brent Olsen was on duty and came out to say hi.

"Hey, Brent!" Johnny said, getting out his wallet.

"Hi, Johnny. Takin' 'er out for a little spin today?"

"Thought we'd give it a try. Looks kind of rough out there."

"The wind's startin' to pick up. Shouldn't get too bad though—sun's warmin' things up."

"Many boats out today?"

"Nah. Too early in the season. A few guys fishin' is all. They caught a three-pounder yesterday. You bring your gear?"

"Not this time. We just came up to waterski."

"Waterski! Water's pretty cold for waterskiin'. Unless you got a wetsuit or somethin'." He laughed.

"No, just thought we'd check it out."

"Well, good luck. Stop back on your way out."

Brent gave John a wave and we drove to the boat ramp. Putting the truck in neutral John eased it backward down the ramp until the trailer was in the water. I was walking the kids over to a cement pad where they would be out of the way, when I heard John holler.

"Whooooeee!"

I turned around to see him up to his knees in the water.

"It's freezing!" he said.

"I *knew* it would be cold," I said.

"Well, you were right. It's pretty darn cold! My feet are going numb." And he started to unhitch the boat.

I situated the kids on the cement pad and went to help him, doing what I could to stay out of the water. He came around on the other side.

"Have you seen the mooring line?" he asked. "It's not here."

The mooring line was a piece of thick, white, nylon rope tied to the bow of the boat. It had always been my job to stand in the water and hold the boat by the line while John drove the truck and trailer up out of the water. The line had never been missing before.

"No. I haven't seen it."

He looked around for it and finally said, "Oh, well. It's okay. I'll hold it while you park the truck." He threw me the keys.

I parked, grabbed the picnic supplies, and locked the truck. In the meantime, John had pushed the boat over to a low T-shaped dock and came to help me. He headed for the boat, his arms loaded with picnic supplies. I followed, carrying Clint and holding Michael's hand. Jennifer walked in front of me.

We walked to the water's edge and then across the wobbly boards of the dock toward the eighteen-foot boat. Its white hull gleamed in the sun and its yellow seats seemed to cheerfully invited us aboard.

"Everybody in!" John said as he climbed into the boat.

One by one, I handed the children to him, then climbed in myself. The boat rocked in the unsettled water. The wind may have picked up even since we arrived.

We donned our life jackets, I double-checked the kids and planted them in their seats. John started the boat, and we eased away from the dock. A moment later, he opened the throttle wide and with a roar of the engines we flew east across the green lake.

The shoreline receded behind us and John turned the wheel a few times to the left and to the right, getting a feel for how the speeding boat played in the water. The waves made a bumpy go of it, but John was handling the craft well. He was in his element, a look of pure content-ment on his face.

We turned to the south towards the dam, keeping an eye out for small bays where the lake might be protected from the wind. But we found no break in the rough waters and after a while arrived at the south side of the lake having had no luck. There, we saw a few fishing boats but no speed boats, and certainly no skiers.

"I don't know, John." I said. "I think the water's just too choppy and cold." I had a growing feeling that we should all stay out of the water today.

He looked a little disheartened, but whipped the boat around heading back north. "Let's try the other side of the lake," he said.

Soon we passed the ramps where we had launched the boat and began exploring new territory beyond. But the water was too rough there as well.

By now I thought we had seen enough to know we weren't going to find smooth water and I said so. But John would not give in. Determined to find a suitable spot, he turned east and partly out of frustration made the boat go even faster. It bounced over the water and the sound of wind and engines roared in our ears. The kids were having a great time. Water shot up from the sides of the boat and into their faces. They laughed and urged John to "go faster, Daddy, faster!"

As the boat slammed down over the waves, the jolt-ing brought back my morning sickness. I had to get out of

that boat and onto firm ground soon. Finally, we reached
the northeast side of the lake, where there was a favorite
cove we had used before for swimming and picnicking. I
pointed to it and said, "This looks great, let's stop here.
Maybe we can ski later if the wind dies down."

John turned sharply toward shore and throttled
down. I knew he was disappointed, but he was a good
sport and made it fun for the kids.

"Here's our favorite place!" he said. "Who wants to
play in the sand?"

"I do!" they shouted and by the time we had eased
into the cove they were out of their life jackets and ready
to jump ship.

John climbed out into the waist-deep water. He shouted,
complaining of the cold with almost every step. He made his
way to the front of the boat and, taking hold of the bow,
pulled us towards shore until the boat's hull hit bottom.

Grateful to be grounded on something solid again, I
herded the kids toward the front of the boat and handed
them down to John. Then I went back for the life jackets.
I was about to throw them out onto the shore when the
impression came: "You won't need these. The water is too
cold. No one is going to swim or ski today." And indeed,
I didn't *want* anyone swimming or skiing. I felt strangely
alarmed at the thought of it, and I left the life jackets right
there on the floor of the boat.

After handing down the food, toys, and the water jug,
I let John help me off the boat. As my feet hit the shallow
water, I screamed. The sharp bite of the icy water sent me
scurrying to dry ground.

Off to one side of our secluded little beach were some
scrubby trees. They afforded some shade and a break
from the wind. So, I carried over our supplies and started
to lay them out. Baby Clint was already starting a sand
castle with the help of his sister, and Michael, a little
sportsman at the age of three, was kicking a ball across
the sand. John was standing there looking out over the
water. I knew he would be weighing the possibilities that
conditions might improve enough to give him a chance
to ski.

Suddenly John spotted a fish among some rocks near
the shore and called out, "Michael! Come quick. A fish!"

Michael left his ball and went running.

"It's a big one. Hurry!"

John grabbed a stick and the two of them chased the
fish, trying to spear it. John was acting like a kid, whooping it up, splashing through the water. He wanted to "catch
a big one" for Michael. Maybe he thought we wouldn't go
home without *some* success after all.

I stood up and watched their antics. They almost
had him a couple of times, but the fish was too fast and
got away.

"Let's find another one, Dad," I heard Michael say.

Then I noticed the boat. It had slipped free from the
soft sand and had floated about a boat's-length away from
shore.

"John!" I called. "The boat! It's floating away!"

John turned and looked.

"Maybe you'd better bring it higher up on shore," I
suggested. The water was so rough now that only by

pushing the boat up high on the beach would we be sure not to lose it. It would be a long walk around the lake to the ranger's station if the boat slipped away. A *long* walk.

That missing mooring line, I thought. We could have used it to tie the boat to a tree.

John was getting ready to wade out after it. He took off his shirt, handed it to me, and started in. In sympathy, I seemed to feel the cold myself as he pushed through the icy water, and I shivered.

Just then the wind swelled and the boat drifted a little farther out. The increasing waves made it bob up and down in the water. When John reached the place where the boat had first drifted, it had moved farther out into the lake.

Hurry, John, I thought. It's getting away.

A few more steps and John came to the edge of the drop and had to start swimming. I imagined the shock as he plunged his bare upper body into the freezing lake.

"Swim, swim!" I called. The wind was blowing harder now and the boat was drifting fast.

He can make it, I thought. John was in great condition and was a powerful swimmer.

He was nearing the boat and I called out my encouragement. "Go. Go! You're almost there!"

Reaching out, it seemed he could almost catch the boat, but the wind and the waves drove it out of reach. With a loud bellow he pumped up his energy against the cold and swam faster. Again it seemed he would overtake the boat when again the wind forced it back. The waves were growing higher now and sometimes I lost sight of him in the rough water. By now I could see that his body was red with the cold and I knew he must be numb all over. If only he could reach the boat and climb into it and out of the freezing lake.

He kept up the chase for what seemed like several minutes, the receding boat luring John farther out into the lake. "Keep going! You can do it!" I coached, but I was starting to think that maybe he should quit trying and head back to shore, except that losing the boat would be troublesome for us. My heart was beating wildly and I paced back and forth on the sand as I yelled encouragement to him.

John bellowed again; he had to keep his energy up to fight the cold. I knew my husband was not a quitter. When he went for something, he battled all odds to achieve his goal. He *would* be able to do this, I reassured myself.

I saw that he was finally within reach of the boat, but it pitched back and forth in the waves and he couldn't grasp the high sides to pull himself up. I thought again of the mooring line and cursed its absence. How easily John might have caught hold of it early on and towed the boat to shore.

The wind and the current again drove the boat out of his reach. John fought to keep up. I was alarmed to see how far out he was by now. It would be a long swim in this cold water if he had to leave the boat and make his way back.

Then I noticed John's movements. They were notably sluggish and misdirected. In horror I realized that my husband was in trouble. Hypothermia. A condition that results when the internal body temperature falls below normal. What were the symptoms? Drowsiness, mental confusion, unconsciousness. My dread deepened. I looked and saw that the boat was now many yards from where John was struggling in the waves and knew that he clearly needed my help.

I ripped off my shorts and shirt and, with only my swimsuit as a thin barrier against the cold, started into the lake. The full measure of the icy temperature slammed into my body like a million freezing needles. Two strokes, three strokes, I plunged in and pulled myself toward John. My mind reeled as I felt my hands and feet go numb. It was worse than I could have imagined. It was as if I were swimming through heavy bricks of ice that bruised my arms with every stroke. I started to kick and felt my legs heavy and unwilling to respond. My heart pounded in my chest as I recognized what it must be like for John who had been in this water far longer. I became terrified.

An intense prayer rushed through my mind. Oh, please, Heavenly Father, give me strength to save him. Just help me get to him. I will need a miracle to drag him back to shore.

I kept swimming, forcing my arms and legs to push onward. The wind ravaged the water around me, making progress more difficult.

I've got to save him, Heavenly Father. I love him. I need him with me forever. Please, please, help me!

I looked up to see where John was. I was only a quarter of the way there. The waves and the current seemed to be pulling him farther away from me. His movements were slow and aimless. I could see he was fighting just to keep his head above water.

"Keep swimming, John. Keep moving!" I yelled and then prayed again. Help me reach him in time. I'm not a strong swimmer. I'm out of shape and I'm pregnant, Father. Please protect us. Give me the strength and the power. I know I can save him with thy help.

Suddenly, something stopped me in my course, and I was lifted in the water by a powerful force and thrust backwards towards the shore. A strong impression asserted itself into my mind. "Chris, go back! There is nothing you can do for John. Your children need you, Chris. Now!"

I turned toward my children on the shore and saw eighteen-month-old Clint chin-deep in the freezing water. He was trying to get to me. Jennifer and Michael were in the water too. They were all crying, "Mommy, Mommy!" In that moment, under the influence of that heavenly spirit, I sensed that Melanie and Stephanie were somehow there too, in some way connected to this scene and in need of my help. An image of the growing child within me filled my mind. I was flooded with the knowledge that, at that very moment, my children needed me. All six of them. Their lives depended on my survival! I also knew that I could continue swimming and probably still reach John, who in this dire moment so desperately needed my help. But I knew with a certainty that if I swam to him, I would die with him. My heart tore asunder as I knew what I must do. I glanced back at Johnny, and crying out in wrenching despair, I struggled back towards shore.

Tears flowed as I swam. Maybe there was still hope. Please, Heavenly Father. *You've* got to save him now. And I swam for all I was worth.

When I reached the shore, I pulled Clint and the other two out of the water. I carried them up a little hill and sat them down. I told them not to move, then ran frantically back to the water to do what I could for John. I went out as far as I could and still touch the bottom. Desperate to help him, to hear his voice, I was compelled to get as close to John as I could. My body was now so frozen that I couldn't feel anything. My skin was reddening and felt like leather. My limbs seemed disconnected except that I could feel my legs starting to cramp. But I stayed there and yelled for help. I thought I heard the sound of a motorboat, but I couldn't see one. I also yelled to Johnny. I could see him out there trying to swim again, but he was headed in the wrong direction.

"Swim to me, John. Swim to *me!* Tell me what to do!" I thought if he could make it half-way, maybe somehow I could reach him. But I remembered the unborn child. I did not want to threaten its life. The water was so cold.

I kept watching John and calling to him. His body was bright red now. His limbs were stiff. And then suddenly, he stopped swimming. The wind and the waves had intensified. He disappeared for a moment, and when I could see him again he was floating on his back. John had been an Eagle Scout. He knew what to do when in trouble. He was survival floating to try to save himself. And then I heard his voice.

Above the roar of the waves and the wind, I heard him call my name.

"Chris. I'm dying," he said. "I'm going to die."

I cried, "No, you are not! You're not going to die. You're going to swim to me, Johnny! You're going to make it! Please try."

"I love you, Chris. We'll be together again . . ."

I can never describe what I felt in my heart, standing in the mouth of that cove, chest deep in the deadly waters—my children crying behind me on the top of a hill. Helpless and alone, I watched my beloved husband sink beneath the waves. Icy water closed over his chest, his face, and he disappeared into the deep.

"Johnny . . ."

Breathless, I waited for him to rise.

"Johnny!"

He did not.

A minute passed. Then two.

And then, to my amazement, the wind became calm. The waves were still. The boat lay suddenly motionless in its place. I was looking over a tranquil, glistening sea of glass. It was the moment of his dying in the dark waters of the lake. I felt his spirit leave his body. I knew when he was gone. . . . And like the waters around me, I became calm. A glowing spirit of comfort enfolded me. I was at peace in that eternal moment of his passing. He was returning to his Father in Heaven. I knew this with clarity: his death was meant to be. He was no longer for this world, but for another. It was his destiny. He was going home.

And I, in that instant, standing in the serene waters of Yuba Lake, accepted his destiny. As my own.

Chapter Three

"Mommy! Mommy!"

The sound of my children's cries brought me to myself.

Energy surged through my body. My children needed me. I spun and charged back to shore, feeling the water's icy grasp with every step. Emerging from the lake, I threw on my shirt and shorts and gathered the children to me.

"Where's Daddy!" Jennifer sobbed.

"He's in the lake, Jennifer. We have to get help." I pictured him, lifeless, sinking down, down. "We've got to run, honey. Can you follow Mommy?"

I pulled Clint and Michael into my arms and stood up. I looked for the boat. It was drifting slowly into the middle of the lake. How far was it to the ranger's station? Three, four miles? It didn't matter. In spite of the weight of two children in my arms, I felt I could have run a marathon. Without giving a thought for our things on the beach, I made sure Jennifer was with me, and then we headed northwest along the curve of the shore.

As we ran, I frantically kept an eye out for anyone I could shout to for help. We ran a hundred yards, two hundred yards, a quarter-mile. I saw no one. Once, I heard a boat, but couldn't see it.

"Someone help us!" I cried.

No response.

I agonized. Why did we have to come today? It's April! The lake is deserted.

As we ran, a thousand images tumbled through my mind. Did I really witness my husband drown? Could it be true? I went over the scene again and again in my mind. The wind. The boat. John swimming. The waves. John sinking. I cried out in my mind, He can't be dead! I mustn't give up hope! I've got to find help; maybe there's still a chance. Miracles *do* happen. Heavenly Father, send a miracle.

Keep running, I told myself.

Jennifer was crying. The fine sand made it hard for her to keep up. "Run, Jennifer, run!" I encouraged her. The boys were awkward in my arms and I shifted them, settling them over my hips on each side.

This was crazy. What was I doing? How was I going to make it back to the ranger station on foot with three tiny children in tow? I felt panicked. I couldn't bear to think of John submerged in the dark, icy water. I needed him out, now!

I pushed on, walking now, but moving as briskly as I could. We soon came to a place where the shore jutted out forming a craggy bluff and blocking our way. To get past it we would have to swim around it or climb to the top of the ridge of jagged mounds that ran along this side of the lake. It would not be as easy as walking along the water's edge but I refused to try swimming around the bluff. We found a little path and climbed to the top of the low ridge. From on top, I could see farther and searched the lake for boats. There were none.

We moved on, dodging rocks, sagebrush, and the occasional scrubby cedar growing along the ridge. My skin and clothes were drying, and I was beginning to feel the heat of the sun. The rough ground burned our feet, and I wished that we had stopped to put on our shoes.

How far we'd gone I didn't know. I just wanted to get to that ranger station and bring help back for Johnny. But progress was getting difficult. Clint and Michael were restless from jostling on my hips. I stopped and traded sides, positioning them for better balance. They clung to me as best they could, grasping my shirt in their fists.

"It's okay, boys," I said. "We'll find someone soon to help us. Hold on to me."

By my mood I think they understood the seriousness of the situation and didn't complain much. Did they understand what had occurred? Clint could not have, but Michael knew something had happened to his dad. His little jaw was set and his eyes were moist. Fear was in Jennifer's eyes. My precious young ones, I thought. What was I going to do? "Come on, guys," I said. "We can make it. Daddy needs us to hurry." We continued on.

Soon, my arms ached from carrying both boys and I stopped to put Michael down. "Can you hold Jennifer's hand and walk fast like Mommy?" I asked him. He nodded his head, yes.

Jennifer was tired, her little face streaked with tears. "How much farther?" she wanted to know.

"It's still a long ways." I knew the west end of the lake was still far off. "Can you help your little brother to make it?"

She nodded. "Mom?"

"What, honey?"

"Did Dad die?"

I knelt down and looked into her blue-gray eyes. "Yes," I said softly, feeling my heart break. "He died in the water, trying to get the boat." And then I cried and hugged her and told her that everything would be all right. "Heavenly Father will take care of us," I said. "He'll watch over us and send us the help we need." In that moment with Jennifer, a lifetime of believing that God is there, that he loves and cares for us in times of trouble, bore fruit. I was able to say to her what my parents had so often said to me. And the words had meaning and emotion and truth behind them. And I realized I had said them as much for myself as for her.

I stood and we started again. Heavenly Father, I silently prayed, I know you're there. Help us make it. Send someone to us. We need thee, Father. Show me what to do.

I had never before uttered so many intense prayers in so short a time. My heart cried out for assistance from above. My body was on automatic—moving forward without direction from my mind. My feet were in motion and my body was doing its job to keep them that way, getting energy from some unknown source. But it was a battle to keep my mind focused in a constructive way. My emotions reeled. Losing John was more than I could take in. My mind coursed with a thousand rampant thoughts—trying to sort through what had happened, to attach order to it, make sense of it; attempting to work out what to do next, how to remain responsible, how to see my children through; worrying that I was doing the wrong thing, moving in the wrong direction, missing something critical to our safety. And so I resorted to prayer, repeating over and over requests for heavenly aid. Praying focused me and kept the terror of despair at bay, and soon I recognized my prayers were being answered. Support came. I felt sustained and knew I was not alone. I was comforted and assured that we would make it through.

We continued along the row of rugged mounds that followed the wide bend of the shoreline. The sandy dirt beneath our feet was strewn with sharp rocks and stickers and we had to stop often and pull them from our feet.

Finally we came to tire tracks that headed north, away from the lake. I knew they must lead to the main road which would take us to the ranger station. Even though that trail was rocky and pitted, taking it would be easier than traveling along the shore. Maybe we'll catch a ride to the station, I thought. There were bound to be vehicles on the main road. Please, Father, let there be someone on the road when we get there—someone to take us where we need to go.

We turned and followed the tracks. They wound through low dusty mounds covered with sagebrush and tumbleweeds. The going was a little easier at first, though it wasn't long until we were hot and covered with sweat and dirt. Another half-mile and my arms were cramped from carrying Clint; Jennifer and Michael barely dragged along. It was all I could do to keep them moving ahead.

We walked for what must have been another twenty minutes and I was coming to the end of my endurance. Clint was like lead in my arms. How much farther to that road? I stopped, feeling that if I took one more step, I would fall to my knees. The sun was high overhead, and I wondered how long it had been since we left the cove. We'd been walking a long time. The wind had come up again, and we were moving against it. The air was filled with swirling dust. The children were coughing and crying and complaining of thirst. My own throat was parched and I scolded myself for having left the water jug behind. How foolish I had been!

Then my mind was filled with turmoil. Had I been foolish during John's accident too? Was there something I could have done to prevent it? Should I have convinced him *not* to go after the boat at all? Could I have thrown him something, perhaps? A rope . . . but there was no rope. A life jacket . . . but I had left the life jackets in the boat. Maybe Michael's ball. John could have used it to stay afloat. But could I have thrown it that far? And the wind. Why the wind? Oh, Johnny, Johnny. Could I have saved you? Should I have tried to swim to you after all? And then I thought of John's parents. What will I say to them, John? How will I tell them? They love you so much. You've got to help me. Guide me, Johnny. I'm lost. My strength is gone. Show me the way.

Suddenly, like a strong fresh breeze clearing away morning mist, words entered my mind with a force and clarity that chased away doubts and confusion. They were spoken in the warm cadence of my husband's soothing voice.

"Chris," he said. "This was meant to be."

My heart was filled with his presence. John was near my side.

"You'll be fine," his voice continued. "The Lord has promised it. He said if I returned to do his work on the other side, he would watch over my family. The Savior will bless you, Chris. You must trust him and listen to his promptings."

A feeling of peace washed over me, and I felt an overwhelming love for my husband. It was *his* comfort, *his* support I had felt throughout our long walk. John had been there for us every step of the way. Tears of gratitude fell on my cheeks. Thank you, John. Thank you, Lord, for letting John be with us.

I raised my head. Was that the sound of an engine? I looked and saw a black pickup truck traveling south along the hills near the lake. The main road! I quickly set Clint down and ran. The truck carried a full load of hay and was moving slowly so as not to upset its load. If I hurried I could catch it before it passed. I ran as fast as I could, arriving just before the truck did. I waved my arms and yelled, but it continued on. No, I prayed. Please, stop! I waved again and the truck slowed, then stopped. I ran to the cab and the driver got out. He was an older man dressed in overalls.

"Thank you for stopping," I said. "I've had some trouble. Could you give me a ride to the ranger station? My husband has drowned in the lake."

"Your husband has drowned?" Alarmed, he turned to his wife who was still sitting in the truck.

"How did it happen?" she asked as she climbed out.

"He was swimming, trying to catch our boat. The water was so cold. I couldn't save him. I have my children with me." I turned and saw them coming down the road, Jennifer and Michael on either side of Clint, holding his hands, keeping him from tripping over the ruts. "Could you take us to the station? I've got to get help."

"Oh, dear. Of course. Let's get going," this good woman said, and helped me gather the three children into the cab.

Chapter Four

*W*ith everyone situated in the truck we headed for the ranger station. I learned that the man and woman were the Monroes from Scipio. They showed so much concern for me, and Mrs. Monroe spoke so sweetly to the children. "You have such a cute little brother," she said, trying to keep Jennifer and Michael calm. I felt comforted being with her. The ranger station was not far, but Mr. Monroe was driving slowly, and now that we had a ride, I was more anxious than ever to get to the ranger station. I became frustrated.

"Please, hurry!" I said. "I've got to get help."

He sped up a bit and we continued steadily on. The children were quiet, exhausted from our hike. It was good to be sitting down.

I told the Monroes in more detail what had happened, but I was more anxious to get to the ranger station than I was to talk. It had been over two hours now, but it seemed far more. Had time stopped? My grasp on reality was slipping. I knew my husband's death was a fact, but I still felt an urgent need to get help for him. My mind knew it would do no good, but my heart couldn't accept that. I could never give up on him.

In a few minutes we arrived at the ranger station—a minuscule white and green trailer with a Coke machine out front. Across the lot sat our truck. I ran up to the door and knocked.

A park ranger answered.

"I need your help right away," I pleaded. "My husband has drowned. Please, you have to help me."

"What is your name?" he asked.

"Chris Monsen and my husband is John."

"Where did this happen, Mrs. Monsen?"

"On the north side of the lake. There's a little cove."

"Are you sure he, uh, drowned?" He spoke the word reluctantly, as if it would cause me pain.

"Yes. He went under and I couldn't get to him. He never came up. Could you take me in a boat to find him?"

"All right. I'll notify the sheriff's department, and then it will take a few minutes to get the boat into the water." He saw my panic and in an effort to calm me placed his hand on my arm and said, "My name is Shon Tripp. We'll get you the help you need, Chris." Then he turned to use the two-way radio.

"Thank you," I said. "Please, hurry."

There was a pay phone outside the trailer. I would now have to use it to do one of the hardest things I had ever done—call Lewis Monsen, John's dad, and tell him

his son had died. During my long walk I knew I would
have to call somebody in the family once I got to a phone.
A feeling told me not to call my own parents; I later
learned they were away from home. John's mother, Janet,
would be home, but I felt I should call Lewis at work
instead. Somehow I knew he would arrange for the help I
needed, but how I dreaded making the call. Lewis loved
John with the heart of a devoted father. John had even
been named Lewis after his dad, although he'd always
been called by his middle name, John. I knew the news
would crush his father, and I didn't know the right words
to use. I was afraid that telling Lewis would cause me to
lose control—and I had to stay strong for Johnny. I said a
quick prayer to God for courage and to John for guidance
and picked up the phone.

I dialed the operator.

"May I help you?" she said.

"Yes. Operator, I need your help. I don't have any
money and my husband has drowned. Could you dial a
number for me?"

"Of course."

I gave her Lewis's office number at Millard High
School where he was now assistant principal.

When the phone started to ring, I wanted to hang
up. I was trembling with emotion, but I knew I had no
choice; I had to tell John's father.

"Hello?"

My heart wrenched. I feared my legs might collapse.
"Lewis, this is Chris. Can you hear me?"

"Yes, Chris. What can I do for you?"

"Everything," and tears began flowing from my eyes. "Dad, a terrible accident has happened."

"Chris, where are you?"

"I'm at Yuba Lake. John has drowned."

"What? Are you sure? Chris, what happened?"

I described it for him. "The boat drifted off the shore and the wind was blowing so hard that the boat got away from him. The water was too cold and he . . . couldn't swim anymore. Dad, I tried to help him, but I couldn't. I'm so sorry." I was overcome by tears. "Can you send help?"

"Yes. Deputy Sheriff White is here in my office. He just spoke at an assembly. We'll send help right away." There was a moment of silence. "Chris, you're sure he's . . . gone?"

"Yes, Dad. I'm sorry. I watched him go under and waited for him to come back up, but . . ."

Shon walked over and indicated that the boat was ready.

"Dad," I said. "I have to go. The park rangers are taking me out to see if we can find Johnny."

"Okay, Chris. Sheriff White says he'll head up there himself. Can you come back with him, or should we come get you?"

"No, don't come. I'll be all right. Thank you, Dad. I have to go."

We said good-bye and hung up.

It hurt to have borne such devastating news to John's dad. Now this was a day of tragedy not only for me and my children but also for John's father. Soon, his mother would know, then my parents, and then our brothers and sisters and their families. I visualized the news rippling out and felt anguish with each succeeding wave.

"Sure you're up to this?" asked Shon as we walked to the boat.

"I can do anything if you promise to get him out of the water," I said.

We climbed into the boat and another ranger, named Kevin Carter, sat behind the wheel and powered it up. We headed out, according to my directions, towards the cove.

Riding in the boat reminded me of our morning's journey across the lake—except that now the surface was calm. My emotions, however, were not. I should never have let Johnny bring us here, I was thinking. Why hadn't I listened to my feelings? Why didn't I make him understand? I had known something was wrong. If I had insisted, maybe things would have been different. Maybe John would still be alive.

These thoughts swarmed through my mind. But they were not edged with guilt. I knew somehow that I could not have changed what had happened. I remembered John's words, "This was meant to be." Still my anguish was not tempered. My insides felt squeezed by a vise and I wanted to lie down in agony in the bottom of the boat and curl up into a ball. The only thing keeping me going was the driving need to find John.

As we approached the cove, I looked for our boat and saw that the wind had pushed it all the way across the lake. It was now resting against the opposite shore.

"There's our boat," I said, pointing it out to Shon.

"We'll get it later," he said. "The important thing is to pinpoint where your husband went under. Then we'll know where to start looking for him. Can you show us the place?"

"I think so." I oriented myself and tried to judge the distance between where we were and the shore. "I think the boat had gotten out farther than this," I said.

I was trying to find other landmarks that might help me orient myself better. I was so anxious to find Johnny that I couldn't relax and think.

"Is this far enough?" Kevin asked, letting up on the gas.

This wasn't going to work. I had been watching John from near the shore looking out, and we were out on the lake looking in. It was difficult for me to judge. "It seems like he was farther out, but I'm not sure."

The boat nudged farther out into the lake.

"How's this?" he asked.

"It's probably close," I said, but I wasn't sure at all. This was so frustrating. Nothing looked familiar. It was as if the lake were playing tricks on me, shifting things until I couldn't tell where we were. I went to the side of the boat and peered into the water. The surface looked sinister and slippery, the water cloudy from the wind. Somewhere down there in that dark water was my husband's body, floating in the depths, or lying on the bottom. It seemed to me he wouldn't be that hard to find, if only we could get down to him.

"Can't you just get in the water and find him?" I pleaded. "I'm sure he's near here."

"Chris," Shon said. "The water is thirty-two degrees.

That's freezing! No one can go in without a wetsuit and scuba gear. It's too dangerous."

"But don't you understand?" I cried. "I can't bear to have him down there." I felt so helpless. I was panicking. "Why can't I do something to get him out!"

"You *are* doing something, Chris. Everything that *can* be done at this point. There are methods to search for somebody in the water. We have to set up a grid for the rescue teams, and you're giving us a place to start. That's the only way to find him."

So, I would have to see Johnny's rescue put off, I thought. I had envisioned coming out here and just pulling him from the water. It should have been that simple. I was expecting that. I hadn't considered how I would *feel*, seeing his body—I hadn't thought even that far ahead. I just knew I had to *get him out*. Then I would move on, deal with what came next. But things were getting complicated, blocking my efforts to help John. It wasn't going to be simple after all. I had to surrender myself to the reality that it was going to take time.

And so, for the second time that day, I was forced to abandon my husband to the water. I forced my panic aside by concentrating on what I needed to do. "Please, take me to the shore," I said softly. "Maybe I'll be able to see things better from there."

We idled up to the shore. Shon helped me out and I took him to the spot I had entered the water to go after Johnny, showing him the direction I had swum. He communicated with Kevin by walkie-talkie to line up the boat until I thought it was in the right place. By now, other boats had arrived and rangers and Search and Rescue people had disembarked and were transferring equipment to the shore.

As they worked they asked me: "How far did John swim past the drop-off?" "What direction was he swimming at first?" "How fast was he going?" "What direction was the wind blowing?" "Did the boat change course as it drifted?" Uncertain, I tried to answer their questions accurately enough to be truly helpful. I was the only source of information that could lead the rescuers to Johnny.

Soon police cars arrived at the lake's edge. An officer emerged from one of them and came up to me. He introduced himself as Sheriff Dave Carter of Juab County.

"As sheriff of this county," he said, "I will be in charge of the search and rescue operation here. I know this is hard for you, Mrs. Monsen, and I'm truly sorry. But, I need to ask you some questions that will help us find your husband and to file an official report."

I nodded, and he began his questions. I tried to give him complete answers but it was difficult to concentrate with the swirl of activity surrounding me. What had been a private calamity was now a public drama. The mechanisms that society had set up to handle such things were taking over. I was not so much comforted by this as I was frightened and overwhelmed. This was the man I loved. He was my life's intimate companion. I had been charged by the heavens to care for him, and my power to do so was being stripped from me. I was not being rendered powerless by choice or even by society, but by circumstance. The deep, cold waters dividing me from my husband created a chasm I could not cross.

"About what time did you notice the boat had drifted away from the shore, Mrs. Monsen?"

"I don't know. It would have been . . . I don't know." I put my hands to my face.

Then I felt a hand on my shoulder and turned to see Deputy Sheriff White. He had made it from Holden.

"Chris," he said and took me in his arms. "I think you've had enough." He asked Sheriff Carter if the questioning could continue later. I felt suddenly comforted by Garth White's compassion, by his recognition of my needs. "The scuba teams will be here soon," he said to me. "Let's go get your children and take you home."

"My children!" I cried. I was horrified that I had not thought of them since arriving at the ranger station. I am a careful mother. I know where my children are at all times. That I had let *anything* blank out all thought of them was appalling. It revealed my true mental and emotional state and I was scared. Yes, I thought. I *have* had enough. "Where are they?" I asked.

"The Monroes have taken them to their home in Scipio. They're fine."

"Thank you."

"Shon here made the arrangements, and you can thank the Monroes once we get there."

"I will. Just let me gather up our things."

The picnic supplies and play things lay undisturbed on the sand as we had left them earlier. The sheriff picked up the toys while I put away the food, folded the picnic blanket and picked up our shoes and the water jug we had needed so desperately on our morning trek. Suddenly I noticed something in the sand near the water's edge. It was John's shirt. I picked it up, and my emotions finally flooded over. I stood there holding Johnny's shirt to my face and sobbed uncontrollably.

Chapter Five

Sheriff White helped me to his car and we pulled away. Following a dirt road, we eventually connected with the tracks my children and I had followed earlier. When we arrived at the main road, I was surprised to see how far we had traveled that morning.

The ride south to Scipio went quickly. I felt bewildered riding in the passenger seat of a sheriff's sleek car. I stared at the rifle in the rack and listened to the crackly voice of the radio dispatcher. I knew, of course, that Sheriff White's job was to involve himself in people's crises. It felt strange that this one was mine.

When we arrived at the Monroe home, Mr. Monroe was waiting for us at the door. "Hello, Sheriff, Mrs. Monsen," he said and led us in.

The living room was small. Flowery slipcovers dressed up a simple couch and chair. Sitting on the braided rug were Jennifer and Michael. Mrs. Monroe stood near the window with Clint in her arms.

"Mommy!" Jennifer said, and she and Michael jumped up and ran to me.

"Here I am," I said, pressing them to me.

Clint started crying. He reached for me.

"Oh, my baby." With the others in tow, I went to him and took him in my arms. "Mommy's here. It's okay."

"He slept for a little while," Mrs. Monroe smiled.

"Oh, thank you," I said and immediately teared up. "I'm so sorry. I didn't mean to just...walk off and leave them." I started crying. "I don't know what I was *thinking*!" I couldn't say anything more.

"I understand," she said and helped me to the couch. "You've had a terrible shock. I probably would've done the same thing." Mrs. Monroe continued, "I washed them up, and we had some lunch. They've been calm most of the time. I don't think they really understand what's happened."

I hugged Clint and wondered how I would ever help them understand. They'd lost their daddy—a fact *I* couldn't even comprehend.

In a few minutes we were ready to leave. I thanked the Monroes again, feeling immense gratitude and relief that such trustworthy and caring people had come along to help. I knew that the Lord had sent them in their slow-moving truck, like angels, to assist us.

We got into the sheriff's car; this time I sat in the back with my children. I waved good-bye out the window to the Monroes standing side by side on their porch, and we headed for Holden. The drive would be a short fifteen minutes, but I dreaded our arrival and wished the trip were longer. I would soon face John's parents and I was not prepared. John was so loved by his family—his loss would pierce their hearts. How could I witness his parents' grief and not dissolve into a mass of emotion myself? I wanted to maintain control, to describe the accident and answer questions to their satisfaction, but I felt incapable of it. I was worried they might think it was my fault John had died, though Shon and Sheriff White had assured me it could not have been. My only solace, witnessed to me by John himself, was that his death was meant to be—that it had purpose. This could be his family's solace, too, if I conveyed it properly. I only hoped they would accept it.

"Where shall I take you?" Sheriff White asked as we left the highway and entered Holden.

"To Lewis's. My daughter Stephanie will be there."

When we drove up to the big, white stucco house, Lewis came out across the wide lawn to meet me. His face was pale, his eyes anxious behind the dark frames of his glasses. As he drew near the car, a huge lump formed in my throat. It was natural to fall into his arms.

"I'm so sorry, Dad," I said, choking with tears. "I did everything I knew how to do."

"I know you did, Chris," he said. "It's okay."

Janet, John's mother appeared on the porch. A trim woman with a noble bearing, her face was grief-stricken. Jennifer and Michael saw her, jumped out of the car, and ran to her.

"Grandma!" they yelled.

She hugged them and took them inside.

I held Clint while Lewis unloaded our things from the car. He asked the sheriff if there was any new word from the lake.

"Not yet," Sheriff White said. "They've only been out there an hour."

"You'll let us know as soon as there's news, Garth?"

"I will," the sheriff said. "Yuba Lake is in Juab County—that's out of my jurisdiction—but I'll monitor everything as best I can. I should be able to keep you informed."

"Thanks, Garth," Lewis said, "for being there when we needed you."

"You're welcome, Lewis. I'll keep in touch. In the meantime, Chris, I'll go pick up your other daughter at school for you."

He waved and got in his car. We watched him drive away, then Lewis wrapped a big arm around me. "Let's go inside," he said and led me toward the house.

Janet met us at the door and enfolded me in her arms.

"Oh, Chris," she said. "This can't be happening." She drew me into the living room and sat with me on the couch. Lewis followed and took a chair near the window. The air was heavy around us, as if the house itself was aware of the tragedy that had overtaken us. The big home had been witness over the years to times of both joy and sadness as this solid couple raised their family. Lewis and Janet had lost another son, Michael Lewis Monsen, to infant jaundice when he was only five months old. He was their firstborn and his loss had been keenly felt. Michael's hair had been red, so when John was born, it had made Lewis and Janet happy that his was too. John had never known his brother, but we had named our first son Michael, after him.

Stake President Condie and his wife, JoAnn, were there at the house. They were Janet and Lewis's best friends.

"Would you like to lie down somewhere, Chris?" Sister Condie asked.

"No," I said. "Thanks, but I wouldn't be able to rest."

"Chris," said Lewis, "if you feel up to it, maybe you could tell us what happened?"

I nodded, but it was hard to know where to start. All I had wanted to say to them was, "I'm sorry. I'm sorry," over and over again. "I'm sorry for losing Johnny." I felt responsible—he was my companion and I had let him drown. But I had done it because I *had* to. The Lord had given me a clear choice: either swim to John and die with him, or swim to the children and live. No matter how dreadful my choice had been, it was the only responsible one to make.

This thought gave me courage and I started explaining, beginning with the decision to spend the day at Yuba Lake. I described everything as best I could to John's parents. I wanted them to understand it all. I explained the force that prevented me from swimming to John and the choice that presented itself to me. "I could have gone to John, but I would have died with him," I said. "And one more thing... I'm pregnant. I had to think of the baby's life."

They looked surprised at first and then grew somber. We all understood how another child would add to the challenge we faced.

After a moment, Lewis said, "Chris, you did the right thing."

We sat there a moment in almost stunned silence, grappling with something beyond comprehension. I was losing a husband, my children were losing a father, and Janet and Lewis were losing a son. These were hard truths to grasp. Our world had suddenly taken a bizarre and fearful twist and reason eluded us. I could sense that Lewis and Janet were harboring hopes that somehow John was still alive. Even I recognized there was a part of me that still could not give up all hope. But they had not watched him drown as I had. I thought they might believe there had been a mistake, or that John would be found washed ashore and alive somewhere, or that if he were dead that a miracle might occur and their son would be restored. Maybe Lewis was considering his own office in the priesthood and believing that, if righteousness and God's will were on his side, he himself could perform such a miracle. As long as John remained in the cold, preserving waters of the lake, wasn't it possible?

I did not suppress the urge to glance at a clock and try to calculate how many hours it had been since the accident. Was it almost four hours now? I had heard of children pulled from frozen waters after twelve hours, and longer, and surviving. How many hours would it take to foil a miracle? Lazarus lay in the tomb *three days* before the stone was pushed back and a commanding voice called him forth. Was this not possible for John? No, Chris, I told myself. Don't agonize like this. You *know* he's gone. He spoke to you himself and told you why he'd been taken.

"There's something I need to tell both of you," I told them. "Johnny came to me after... his death."

Their eyes widened.

"He told me that this was meant to be, that the Lord had work for him on the other side."

They were silent, weighing my words.

"He came to me on the road from the lake," I continued. "I didn't see him, but I felt his spirit and heard his voice in my head. I felt so peaceful. I knew he was there with me. He said that the Lord would watch over us and guide us. That we needed to trust in Him."

"Oh, Chris," Janet said and fell silent.

I wasn't sure if my words had caused them comfort or pain. Comfort that John's dying was meant to be, or pain that this news had come from the world of departed spirits? Maybe they thought these were the words of a deluded woman, that, in my grief, I had conjured up John's words myself. It didn't matter, I decided. I sensed that something inside these two loving and strong individuals was not ready to give up on their son. Their faith was undaunted. I could not begrudge them their desire to hold onto John for as long as they possibly could. After all, I felt the same.

If only the phone would ring to tell us something of him at the lake, I thought, to end this uncertainty and speculation.

After a moment Janet said, "You'll have to tell Stephanie, Chris."

"She doesn't know?" I asked.

"No. When she got here after school, we sent her out to play without telling her. I'll go and get her."

Oh, no. Lord, I can't do this, I silently prayed. Please help me. Give me strength enough for this.

Telling Stephanie would be only one of many times that I would be forced to deal with the ramifications of John's death. Later, I would sign forms, make arrangements for his body, select a casket, carry out funeral and burial services—all inescapable duties. But none would be more painful than telling my child of the death of her father. Of course my own life had changed that day, but in this moment, I could only see a daughter's life about to change, a fragile innocence about to be bruised. I was her *mother*; I couldn't do it. But because I was, I *had* to. Only a mother's tender love can harm and heal all at once.

When she came in, I pulled her close and told this five-year-old girl that there had been an accident at the lake and that her dad was gone. Her brows furrowed.

"He's gone?" she said.

"Stephanie, Daddy drowned in the water. He's with Heavenly Father now."

"But how could he drown'd, Mommy? Daddy's a *good* swimmer."

"The water was too cold. After a while he couldn't move anymore and he . . . went under, but, Honey, we're going to be all right. I love you so much."

Her eyes filled with tears and she suddenly burst out, "I want Daddy. I love Daddy."

"I know sweetheart. It's going to be hard, but we have to be strong for each other. Can you do that?"

"Okay."

"It's all right to cry, sweetie."

We hugged for a long time.

Garth White arrived with Melanie and I went outside to meet her. I saw the concern on her face and realized how it must have been—the sheriff coming for her at school, driving away in the police car—she was confused and scared. I brought her in and, gathering all the children around me, I told the story again—this time in more detail. Melanie, the oldest, needed more information, but she also understood the consequences better and the news was harder to take.

"No!" she cried. "Mom, what will we do without Daddy?" And she burst into tears in my arms.

That's when my heartstrings broke. The full realization that my children would live out their lives without their father bore down on me with its awful weight. They would not just be without a father, they would be without *Johnny*. He was so tender with the kids, protective, and funny. He was a good father. It would have been a rare privilege to be raised by him.

"Daddy is gone," I said through falling tears. "Heavenly Father has called him home. It's going to be hard, but I will be here to take care of you. And Daddy will be watching over you, too." I stopped to wipe my tears. "You will never be alone," I promised.

The afternoon slipped onward. Every passing minute tugged me further from my husband's life and still no word from the lake. Soon there was a solemn gathering of family at the Monsen home. One by one they had all been notified and, dropping what they were doing, had come home.

All the while, I was jittery with worry. I couldn't keep my hands still. I twisted a hundred Kleenexes into tiny shredded knots as I listened for the phone to ring. Oh, please, bring me word. Find my Johnny. *Find him.*

My parents arrived from Richfield where they had been visiting friends. When I saw them come through the door I ran to my mother's arms. "Mom," I cried. "Mom." I sobbed into her neck.

My father joined the embrace and said, "I'm sorry, Chris. So sorry this had to happen." And a moment later, "How are you?"

I said the simple thing: "I'm fine," and wiped my eyes.

I sat with my parents and quietly shared my experience and answered their questions. Then I told them that I was pregnant.

When my mother cried, "That's wonderful news! This baby will be so special!" my heart filled with joy. And for a moment the glow of love for my unborn child washed away my grief.

"When are you due?" she asked.

"Right before Christmas," I smiled. "I'm five weeks along."

"That's wonderful. A Christmas baby! It will be so fun for you and the kids," she said.

"You know," my dad said. "I had it all figured out. I knew you were pregnant."

"You did?" I asked. "How did you know?"

"I can tell. You act differently when you're pregnant. I've been waiting for weeks for you to break the news!"

"Oh, sure, Dad!" and I laughed for the first time since the accident.

Suddenly I felt sick to my stomach and realized I hadn't eaten all day. Janet brought me a plate of food and I gratefully ate a few bites.

As the news of the drowning spread through town, friends stopped in to show their sympathy and to lend their help. This calamity was theirs too, for no life such as Johnny's passes on in isolation. There were many who felt its sting. I embraced each one who came and accepted their tears and their love.

My best friend, Lorna Stevens, arrived, and we hugged and cried.

"I called and told Roger," Lorna said. "We're heart-broken, Chris." Her husband Roger was getting to be great friends with John, and the four of us had spent good times together. Now the two men's friendship would be cut short. John had said to me just the night before, "Of all our friends in Holden, Roger and Lorna are the most humble, sincere, and Christlike. I know they'll make it to heaven. I hope I can be like them."

Lorna stayed by my side, comforting me.

Soon, I heard the phone ring. A minute later Lewis solemnly relayed the news from the lake: "Sheriff Ed Phillips says the scuba teams are just getting started. There's no sign yet of John."

This filled me with renewed anxiety. I loathed the image in my mind of John suspended at the bottom of the lake, lifeless and beyond my help. It was beginning to appear that he was beyond *anyone's* help, beyond rescue. Please, Lord, I prayed. Help them bring him home to us. My anxiety flowed into impatience and I realized I couldn't just sit there and wait. I needed something to keep me busy. I asked my mom and dad to help get my things and take me and the children home. After the long, tiring trek around the lake, I badly needed a shower and a change of clothes.

We lived just around the corner, but we loaded everyone into my parents' car and drove. Mom and Dad were so good. They spoke to the children about school, fussing over them, doing their best to keep things as pleasant as possible in the face of our tragedy. For a moment I felt their efforts even lightening my own burden. But as we approached our house, I looked at it sitting there, our fine little home that John had helped build, and my heart became flushed with sadness. I remembered that when we drove away that morning, it was with excitement and happy anticipation. Now, on our return, things were so different ... so tragically different. We were one less, coming home. And the one that was missing was the one who had been the center of everything. How could we be returning home without him? It was impossible. It couldn't be *home* without Johnny. He was the glue that held everything together. How could *anything* continue without him? How could even this house remain standing? Without John, it seemed wrong that anything should remain intact.

Once inside, Mom and Dad took charge of the kids while I went to our bedroom. The familiar rooms were now strangely incomplete. The children's voices, subdued or silent, failed to bring the usual animated spirit into the house.

I was feeling nothing of John's presence now, nothing of his lingering influence. Feelings of deep loss and loneliness were crowding my heart, and seeing John's things in the bedroom made them worse. Here were my husband's clothes, his shoes. His pocketknife and change on the dresser. His fishing pole and racquetball racket in the corner. His scriptures by the bed. Things used, touched, worn by Johnny. Physical echoes of him all around me, waiting for his return to fulfill the measure of their being here. I imagined him walking through the door, sitting on the bed to put on his shoes, then standing and scooping up the change, dropping it into his pocket, grabbing his scriptures, and heading out again. He'd done it a thousand times. What I would give to see him do it again.

I sat down and buried my face in my hands. Chris, I told myself, hang on to reality. He won't be coming back.

But somehow I was not able to give up completely, at least not while he was lost in the lake. Hope, it seems, is a tenacious thing. Even later, after showering and dressing, with the children gathered in the living room to answer more questions, I spoke in certainty of their father's death, but in my heart the tiniest shred of hope still voiced a prayer for a miracle. When the phone rang, I would hear of it, I believed. Johnny would have been found, somehow alive.

But later that evening when the phone did ring, there was no such news.

"Chris, they've called off the search because of darkness," John's dad said, his voice steady. "They did everything they could, but it will have to wait till morning."

"Okay," I said, trying to show strength though I felt myself crumbling.

"Sheriff Phillips said it may be helpful if you could go up in the morning and show them again where . . . it happened. Do you feel you could do that?"

"Yes, I can do that. I think I would like to. I feel like I need to do *something*. It's so hard . . ."

"I know, Chris. We feel it too. Are you okay? Would you like us to come over?"

"No. Mom and Dad are here. We'll be all right."

"Please call if you need us. I'll be by in the morning about 8:30. Sheriff Phillips will take us up."

"That sounds fine . . . good night."

"We love you, Chris."

"I love you, too."

Afterwards we had family prayer and the kids went right to their beds. They had promised to be my little helpers, and tucking them in, I was buoyed by their courage and their simple faith.

"Are you okay?" Melanie asked. It was the same question she had asked that morning, finding me sick that morning in the bathroom—a scene which seemed so long ago.

"I'm okay, sweetie," I answered. "It's just that . . . it's going to be a little hard on us all until they find Daddy."

"I hope they find him tomorrow."

"I do too, honey. I'm sure they will."

Four-year-old Jennifer said, "Heavenly Father will help us find him."

"Yes, he will," I said. "And then we'll feel better, even though we will be sad too."

I turned out the lights and told them again that I loved them.

Mom and Dad were spending the night, and after a little while we turned in. I was grateful for them. Their presence and their strength was comforting. But once in my room and alone in bed, despair found its way again into my heart. I reached my hand over to John's side of the bed and felt so terribly lost and afraid. The thought that he would be in the lake overnight pierced me to the center and I could not sleep.

Whenever I drifted off, the same dream kept coming, over and over. John was drowning and I was trying to swim to him, to reach him before he went under, but I was always too late. Then I would wake up in a panic and realize that the dream was true–Johnny was gone. He would be in the lake all night long, lying in a deep, watery grave where it was cold, dark, and silent. It was agony to consider that by morning it would certainly be too late for a miracle. My last bit of hope was withering away with the passing night. It was too much to bear, and I sobbed uncontrollably into my pillow.

"Oh, Father," I cried. "I'm all alone. How can I live without Johnny? I love him. I need him. How will I ever manage without him?" And it was this question that I repeated again and again throughout the endless night: how can I live without John?

And finally, gratefully, an answer came.

But not before the blackness of my longest night had darkened every corner of my soul.

Chapter Six

The first light of morning found me kneeling despondently at the side of my bed. The feeling that my life had been destroyed finally came crashing down with all its force, driving me to my knees. I could not live another minute without knowing how I was going to survive without John.

"Heavenly Father," I said, praying more fervently than ever before, "help me go on. I need strength for myself and for my children. If I have to live without my husband, please don't let me live without thee. I can't do it alone. I've got to know how I can make it through." I repeated my prayer again and again, pleading with my Father for an answer.

Suddenly I knew what I should pray for.

"Father," I said, "if only I knew John was happy . . . maybe that would be enough. I just want him to be glad about where he is and happy doing what he is doing. I couldn't bear it if he were missing us and worried and feeling he didn't belong. If I knew he was at peace, then I could be at peace. I could concentrate, control my thoughts and feelings, and go on, do what I need to do. Please, Father. Help me know that everything is okay for John and that he is happy."

As soon as I had said these words, the room filled with a calm beyond compare. The sun burst through the window and bathed my face with light. The Spirit of the Lord came over me with all its warm glow and I felt the Savior's love. The sadness and pain of the night were wiped away. Peace entered my heart. My thoughts became clear, and for an instant I felt in touch with the heavenly realms, and I knew that John was happy! With every fiber of my being I knew his joy and his excitement at being where he was. Hope sprang bright in my heart and gratitude swept through my soul. "Oh, thank you," I said through tears of relief and joy. "Thank you, Father, for hearing me and answering my prayer."

I remained there for a long time, basking in the light and feeling the beautiful glow of what I had experienced. I realized that all I had needed was to know what to pray for. God had shown me and I was filled with wonder and awe at his love.

When I stood up, I knew I had strength enough for the day. I would be going back to the lake to find John's body—a heartbreaking task at best—but no matter how difficult things became, I knew I would make it through.

I dressed and went to the kitchen. Mom was there.

"How do you feel?" she asked.

"Good." I smiled. "I'm not sick this morning for a change." I wanted to keep my experience to myself. It was new and sacred.

"Did you get any sleep?"

"A little," I said, not wanting to worry her. "Lewis will be here soon. Would you mind helping me with the kids?"

"Sure. Let's get them dressed. Breakfast is just about ready."

After breakfast, Mom stayed with the kids and soon Lewis and Sheriff Phillips arrived in the sheriff's Bronco to take me back to Yuba Lake. My dad asked if he could go along. I said I would be grateful.

On the way, I was surprised to feel awake and even able to function, but I didn't feel a trace of morning sickness. I had eaten a good breakfast, and it had tasted delicious—maybe because I hadn't had to cook it.

We drove north on I-15, the same route John had taken yesterday pulling the boat. The four of us rode mostly in silence; it was a serious occasion. I still wanted desperately to find John's body and get him out of that cold lake. Though the task was a grim one, finding him would be a relief to everyone.

Passing Scipio, I said another prayer of thanks that the Monroes had watched over my children while we searched for John. I thought of the failure of that search and prayed that today might be different. I wanted to take the rescue teams right to John. My anticipation grew with every mile. I just knew we would find him. I promised myself I wouldn't leave until we did.

As the Bronco came over the rise, the lake came into view, and my heart rose to my throat. I suddenly remembered how I hated this place. Now I hated it even more. I scanned the lake's surface. "Oh, John," I breathed. "You're in there somewhere..."

At first I saw nothing unusual about the lake. The sun was young in the sky. Its rays reflected on the surface like the day before. It was early and the wind was still calm. A hawk wheeled above the water. No, it wasn't a hawk. It was an airplane. I watched it circle above the near end of the lake and head back to the east. "Is the plane for Johnny?" I asked.

"Yes," answered Sheriff Phillips. "They've called in all the teams from two counties. We're lucky it's early in the season; everyone was available to help."

In the Bronco we easily drove right to the little ridge above the spot where the family had stopped to picnic the day before. The scene astonished me. Vehicles were everywhere along the shore, up and down the lake. Police cars, trucks, station wagons, four-wheel drive vehicles, even a large bus that had transported some of the searchers. Some vehicles were moving along the lake edge, most were parked willy-nilly. Men were everywhere, searching through binoculars atop the mounds of sand, probing along the shore with poles. Equipment was strewn over the ground. Boats of every size and description were dragging ropes and chains behind them, or carrying scuba teams. I was overwhelmed.

"Look at this!" I said. "Who are all these people?"

"Most belong to search and rescue teams from Juab and Millard counties," Sheriff Phillips answered. "We also have a lot of volunteers out today."

"Volunteers?" I asked.

"People who heard the story on the news and wanted to come and help."

It was amazing. The lake was transformed. When we had arrived yesterday morning, it had been deserted. Today there were people everywhere.

Sheriff Phillips took my arm. "We're meeting Sheriff Carter here this morning. He's anxious to go out with you in the boat."

We walked to a motor home parked nearby that served as Sheriff Carter's base of operations. Sheriff Carter came out to greet us.

"Mrs. Monsen," he said, "thank you for coming." Then he introduced me to some other men with him. I could see that my presence made some of them uncomfortable. I wondered if it were standard procedure to include the next of kin in the search for a missing body, or if the men were just embarrassed, not knowing what to say to the victim's wife.

"We'd like you to check things over this morning," he continued, "to see if we're searching in the right spot."

He gave some instructions to the other men and then my dad and I walked with him down to the water's edge. Sheriff Phillips and Lewis remained on top of the hill.

I looked over the lake and noticed some white buoys set far out in the water. A larger, red buoy floated nearer to the shore than the other ones. I asked what it was for.

"It marks the location you identified yesterday as the place your husband went under," Sheriff Carter said. "The other buoys mark the south boundary of the grid area. The boats are working southward out to the white buoys, then turning and coming back north to the shore. As they work, they gradually move from east to west. We've gone over the area many times and . . . we just can't seem to find him."

The red buoy sat in the center of the grid. I watched it bobbing in the water and tried to imagine Johnny in its place, floating there on his back before going under. Was it in the right spot? I walked to the place at the water's edge where I had gone in after him and tried to make a better judgment. Yesterday, I was in no condition to have made a rational determination, and still, it seemed like the buoy *was* in the right place. Then why hadn't they found Johnny? Had they not looked *deep* enough? Or had the wind pushed him out farther than I thought?

"Let's go out again," I said, "to make sure we have the right place. Maybe I'll be able to see it better today."

The sheriff spoke into his radio and a boat wheeled around and came to shore. A breeze was blowing by now, making the water choppy like the day before. As we started out toward the buoy, I felt the wind in my hair and remembered how John had forced the throttle yesterday, sending us speeding across the water. The wind and the spray had pelted our faces. I had felt anxious in the boat without knowing why. Now, of course, I knew, and I wondered why the Lord had not warned us more specifically. With Wilford Woodruff it had been, "Get up and move the wagon" moments before lightning toppled a huge tree. Joseph F. Smith heard the words, "Go in and sit down," and had been spared injury when the train he was travelling in derailed. George Albert Smith was saved from death one dark night when an impression came to "Stop" in his tracks along a high mountain path; one more step would have sent him plunging into the river below. "Don't take the boat out today," would have saved John's life—if only the Lord had spoken it. Or had he tried, and we were too busy with our plans to hear? *No*, I reminded myself before guilt overran me, *this was meant to be.*

We arrived at the red buoy and came to a stop. A wave of emotion came over me; somewhere below us, in this murky green water, was my Johnny. I put my hand to my mouth.

"Are you okay?" My dad moved up behind me.

I nodded, unable to speak.

"Take your time, Mrs. Monsen," Sheriff Carter said.

I felt the boat rocking and thought I was going to be sick. I have to concentrate on why I'm here, I told myself. The rescuers need my help.

I stood up, holding onto the canvas hood of the boat and scanned the shore. I found the spot where we beached the boat, and followed an imaginary line from it to the buoy.

"It seems like the buoy is in the right place," I said.

"Are you sure?" asked Sheriff Carter.

"I can't be completely sure," I said, "but it looks like it is."

I looked around the area and noticed there were boats everywhere except near the red buoy. "You're sure you looked hard enough here by the buoy?"

"Well, like I said," he answered, "we've given it a thorough search. But you have to understand that looking for an object in a deep reservoir, even an object as large as a man's body, is difficult. Even with fancy sonar equipment it's possible to overlook something, what with boulders, tree stumps, and other debris on the bottom."

Something occurred to me and I asked, "If we don't find him, will he eventually float to the surface?"

"The water's cold. It could take a week for that to happen."

I didn't say anything, but looked back across the surface of the water. A couple of men in a boat near the shore were trolling slowly, dragging a rope that disappeared into the water behind them. I knew that at its end there was a bar with sharp hooks affixed to it. A grisly image came to mind of what might happen if sharp hooks came into contact with John's body. I turned away and forced the image out of my mind. *Think of something else, Chris.*

I noticed we had drifted away from the buoy a little. "Could underwater currents have carried him away from here?" I wondered aloud.

"It's not likely. Drowning victims usually go right to the bottom, and in a lake, while there *are* currents, they are usually not strong enough to cause a body to drift. But to cover every possibility, it's standard procedure to start from a central location and set up a grid around it. Then we criss-cross the grid in boats, looking for a hot spot with sonar that might indicate the body and also working with drags. If anyone runs across anything, we send down the divers. The important thing is finding that starting point—the place the victim was last seen—and you've done that for us. Can you think of anything that might cause you to think that this might not be the right spot?"

I shook my head no, but oh, how I wished I could be absolutely sure. I said a silent prayer. Father in Heaven, is there anything I'm missing? Any clue we've passed over? Please help us know where Johnny is, Father. Please! If this is not the right place, *guide me* to the one that is.

As we slowly circled the area in the boat, I went over everything again in my mind. But I didn't feel my thoughts directed in any particular way; nothing new dawned on me; nothing became more clear. I'd thought of it all before, and I remained as doubtful as ever. Now, it seemed, there wasn't anything else I could do, short of going out with a team and searching for Johnny myself— and I knew I wasn't up to that. For some reason, known only to Him, God was not guiding me to John, and I felt helpless. I felt how Johnny might feel were he still inhabiting his body—*lost and alone in this deep, wide lake.*

On the way back to shore I said to my father, "There are so many people out here. Why hasn't someone found him yet?"

"They will, Chris," Dad said. "They'll find him soon. I know they will."

I wasn't as certain. I struggled with feelings of frustration. I felt I should be able to do *more.* "I should have been able to take them right to him," I said.

"You've done all you can do. Maybe we should go back home and trust the searchers to find him."

But I didn't want to leave. How could I leave without Johnny again?

Back on shore, I looked around. More volunteers were arriving. There were sixty or seventy people by now.

Some men nearby struggled to put on scuba gear. Another man, large and blond, was standing barefoot near a car with its trunk open. He was watching a co-worker trying to inflate a raft. Everyone looked so intent on doing their jobs. These men knew what they were doing and they wanted to succeed. Many were probably husbands and fathers themselves. Had they come with the sense of rescuing one of their own? I recognized some of the volunteers as Johnny's friends and co-workers. I watched some new arrivals launching a boat and was surprised to see the tall figure of my oldest brother, Kelly.

"Kelly!" I called and went over to him. He wore a cap over his light brown hair, a jacket, and jeans.

"I came to help," he said solemnly. "I couldn't just sit around."

"I know," I said. "It's hard." Kelly's warm smile always gladdened me. It was so good to see him here.

"Chris . . . I'm sorry." He hugged me. "This is really tough." He looked me in the eyes. "I want you to know that I feel responsible for you in a way. I will do anything I can to help you and your family."

"Thank you, Kelly," I said.

"I know you'd be one of the searchers if you could."

I smiled and dabbed my eyes.

"So, I came instead," he said. "And, Chris, I really want to find him. I want to be the one to find Johnny for you."

Tears spilled from my eyes.

He continued, "I've been praying to be led to him since I was out here yesterday."

"You came yesterday?"

"Yes, in the afternoon. I walked up and down the shore looking for Johnny, thinking that maybe he swam in and you didn't see him because of the waves. Or that he had resurfaced after you left and been washed ashore somewhere, but... I didn't find him." He looked down at the ground and then back at me. "Is there anything you can tell me to help in the search?" he asked.

"That red buoy marks where he went under, but . . ." I hesitated, "maybe he's farther out than that."

"You mean farther south?"

I nodded.

"I'll look there then. Chris, we're going to find him today. I feel that the Lord will help me."

His words filled me with new faith and I said, "I'm sure he will, Kelly."

A feeling of satisfaction poured through me that Kelly, my own brother, would be here representing the family and representing me.

And suddenly I felt that I could leave.

We hugged good-bye and I walked away from the water's edge and back to where Lewis and my dad were standing with Sheriff Phillips and Sheriff Carter. The wind had really picked up and I had to shield my eyes from the blowing sand. I had had enough of this place.

"Okay," I said. "I'm ready to go."

The mood was somber at the Monsen's home when Sheriff Phillips dropped us off. It was early in the day, but all of John's brothers and sisters were there. I saw unbelief and pain in their eyes. Johnny had been the oldest of four living sons and had been a pillar of their family life—they were not ready to give him up.

Some of them had heard only sketchy details of the accident, so I filled in the gaps and tried to help them understand. Answering their questions I sensed in them the same hope I saw in Lewis—that a miracle might yet occur. I realized there was nothing I could say to take this hope away, and maybe that was for the best. Each person would come to grips with John's death in their own way.

A little later, I remembered that today was the day Johnny and I had planned for me to see the doctor and then for the two of us to go to the temple. While there would be no trip to the temple, I became filled with the desire to see my doctor, partly for myself—I wanted that shot for morning sickness—partly for the baby, and partly to follow through on the plans John and I had made. Losing him made me want to carry out every precious decision we had made together that affected our family. My sister Jill took me to the clinic in Fillmore and I received my first prenatal exam for my sixth child.

But first there would be a pregnancy test.

"I *know* I'm pregnant," I said to my doctor, Brent Jackson. "You don't need to give me the test!"

He turned his round, fortyish face to me, "Well, let's do one anyway, Chris. We want to be sure don't we?" He raised one dark eyebrow.

I wasn't up for an argument. I relented and the samples were taken.

While waiting for the results, Dr. Jackson said, "I'm sure sorry about what's happened, Chris. I'm concerned for you. This is not going to be easy."

"No it's not," I said. His caring nature made it easy to cry, and in a moment I was sniffling and dabbing at tears on my cheeks. Actually I had been crying all morning. Knowing John was happy didn't soften my own sense of loss. Every time I thought of John, I cried.

"Chris." He put a hand on my shoulder. "Would you like me to prescribe a sedative to help you through the next few days?"

"No. I don't want to take anything while I'm pregnant," I said.

"That's probably for the best," he said. "But there are some things you need to do whether you are pregnant or not. Take some daily vitamins and get plenty of extra sleep. These next few months are going to be very difficult. Grief can affect the body; you must take care of yourself. When you feel ready for it, you'll need some regular exercise, not only for your body, but to help combat depression."

"Okay, I'll try."

"If there is anything at all I can do, will you call?"

I said that I would.

In a few moments the results came back and Dr. Jackson announced gladly, "Congratulations! You *are* pregnant."

Congratulations, I wanted to say back. Your tests are accurate!

Together we calculated the due date.

"A Christmas baby!" he said. "We'll say December seventeenth. I'm happy for you, Chris."

"I'm happy too," I said. "A little scared, but I'm feeling that this will be a special child."

"We'll keep a close watch on your progress. You've been through this five times already; you know what to expect."

"Let's hope this baby comes with no hitches," I said. There had been a few problems with some of my previous deliveries, and if I had to go through this one without John's support, I wanted everything to go smoothly.

He administered a vitamin B shot for my morning sickness and I left the room.

Jill was in the waiting room. "Well, what's the news?" she asked.

"I'm due in December. The seventeenth."

"Oh, that's wonderful. I'm so happy for you."

I could see that she meant it. But my news brought a different reaction from the other ladies sitting in the room. Glancing at their faces I saw that they pitied me. Fillmore and Holden are small towns; everyone knew me and knew what I was going through. The whole area seemed on edge while the search went on for Johnny. Hearing that I was pregnant only multiplied the tragedy in these women's view. Some only stared at me, unable to say anything. Others were whispering, and I thought, Do they know something I don't? Has John been found? I needed to get out of there.

"Let's go, Jill," I said, and we left.

On the way home I started to feel sick again. The vitamin shots would not take effect for several days. But worse were my recurring thoughts of Johnny. I was in torment every hour that he remained in the lake. It felt like huge wounds were inside my head and my heart that could only be eased by his rescue. How long would it take? I didn't know if I could last.

We returned to my house and I spoke with Sheriff Phillips over the phone.

"There's still no sign of the body," he said.

It sounded so harsh, almost cruel, though I know he didn't mean it that way. The body? No. It was my *husband* they were looking for. Though I knew he didn't inhabit it, his body belonged—even in death—to him. His separation from his body was only temporary. While John himself inhabited the world beyond, his tabernacle of flesh remained here.

"Thank you," I said. "Please let me know as soon as he is found."

"Of course I will, Chris."

I just wanted to get on with this. I wanted John out of that lake and brought back to Holden, wanted to make arrangements for him, wanted to plan a wonderful funeral for him. I wanted to get on with my grieving.

I started to feel angry. I was angry they hadn't found John, angry at the lake, at yesterday's wind and waves, angry at the cold, unyielding water. I was angry at myself for giving in to John and going to Yuba Lake in the first place. I was angry at him for pushing us into it. And then I became angry at my own anger.

What are you doing, Chris? I thought. You had a wonderful spiritual experience this morning. You know that John is happy where he is and that God wants him there. Stop this anger. Control your emotions! But I couldn't control them. It was like I was not connected to myself. One moment I felt angry, the next I felt empty, and the next I hurt so badly I wanted to scream my agony to the world. But I didn't. I kept my worst feelings to myself, and this made me feel disconnected from everyone around me.

All day long people arrived at the house to deliver food and sympathy. Ward members, neighbors, friends. My refrigerator, freezer, and countertops were filled with bread and rolls, salads, and casseroles. Some people stayed only briefly, others lingered, and though I was thankful for their kindness I could not properly appreciate all that was being done for me. I was preoccupied with the search for John's body. There are many times when someone drowns that the body is never found. I didn't want to go through that—not knowing where he was the rest of my life; only a long, wide lake as a place to mourn. I thought there could be so much comfort in a grave site.

By early afternoon all my brothers and sisters had arrived except Tracie who was trying to get a flight out of Nebraska, and Kelly, of course, who was at the lake. Though my brother Ken and his wife Lori had my children, the house was full, and my attention was somewhat occupied with my guests. But as the afternoon crawled on, my anguish continued to grow. I knew John was in the spirit world and was probably pushing ahead in his new existence. Then why couldn't things push ahead here too? I wondered. Why does it have to drag on like this? I knew I couldn't go through another night like the last one. They *had* to find Johnny.

As evening arrived, I was exhausted with my heaving emotions. I was ready to give up and dissolve into a heap of desolation and despair. I would have to do something soon or I would lose control.

Some of the family were leaving to spend the night in their own homes. But I decided to ask for a combined family prayer before they did. I felt our united faith would help them find Johnny and give me strength to endure. I phoned Ken and Lori, and Denise, Kelly's wife, who was also helping with my children, and asked everyone to come to the house. Then I walked to the Monsen home and invited everyone there to come over. They came and soon my living room was filled with all the family, from youngest to oldest. Almost everyone on this earth who was closest to Johnny was there. As we knelt together I looked around and knew the heavens could be moved by these wonderful people. I asked John's dad to say the prayer and everyone bowed their heads in solemn reverence. Even the little ones were silent, feeling the importance of this moment.

"Our Father in Heaven," he began and a powerful spirit distilled upon the room. "Thou knowest why we have come to thee in prayer this day. We who love John Monsen, his wife, his children, his parents and brothers and sisters on both sides of the family, do kneel before thee and unitedly exercise our faith in asking a blessing at thy hand. Father, thou hast called John home. We accept this as thy will. But as his mortal remains have yet to be found, we would ask for thy help that this long ordeal may be brought to an end."

He prayed fervently for John's rescue. He asked for blessings upon the officials in charge and upon the searchers themselves, that somehow they would be led to him. "And Father," he continued, "may it happen soon so that, finally, we will be able to lay our husband, father, brother, and son to rest in a manner befitting his noble and faithful life." These humble words revealed Dad Monsen's heart and reflected the feelings of everyone. During this long wait the family had finally come to accept John's death, to realize he was actually gone, and that there would be no miracle. It was an emotional moment, filled with resignation and sadness. But it was also comforting as we unitedly expressed our love for John to our Father in Heaven and felt God's love for us in return. He asked for blessings of comfort for all the family, for me especially, and for the children. And then he closed in the name of Jesus Christ and everyone echoed the "Amen."

After the prayer there were many tears and expressions of love shared between the two families as we moved outside to say good-bye. We lingered there on the lawn, talking, perhaps unwilling to part. The evening was cool but pleasant under the trees in the yard. I was talking to Robert, one of John's brothers, about their hunting and fishing trips together, and how much John had relished them, when I noticed a police car coming around the corner and knew instantly that they had found John.

The car pulled up, and an officer stepped out. He came directly to me and the family closed around. My heart was pounding like a kettledrum.

"Mrs. Monsen, Sherrif Phillips called from the lake and asked me to come tell you that they've found your husband," he said. "After your visit this morning they narrowed the search area. He was found near the red buoy but farther out. He's in excellent shape. The men that pulled him out said he looked like he could just start breathing again."

My lip started to tremble. "Can I see him?" I asked.

"They're sending him to Juab Hospital before taking him to the mortuary. It might be best to wait till morning and ask the funeral director."

"Thanks for coming to tell us," I said.

"We're all sorry such an unfortunate thing as this has happened," he added.

"Thank you," I said.

"Sheriff Phillips wants you to know that he'll make sure everything is handled properly from our end, that your husband will be well taken care of."

He spoke briefly with John's dad and turned to go, then he stopped. "Mrs. Monsen," he said, "it was the boat your brother Kelly was on that found him."

Kelly, I thought. *Thank you.*

The officer drove away and the family remained outside stunned by the news. It was finally official. John's death was now as real for them as it had been for me. Nothing in them could rationally deny it now and some of them gave in to the grief they had held at bay.

As for me, I could have lain on the ground and wept, but John's brother Robert held me up, and consoled me as I cried. Joy and grief alike encompassed me. The wait was over but something new had begun: life without John. Now that he had been found, we could give him a funeral and then bury him. I thought, We have pulled him from under the water only to lay him under the earth! It was too much to bear. I had lost my Johnny, the person in all the world who mattered most. The agony of it threatened to consume me. It engulfed my mind and gripped my heart with crushing pain.

I hadn't forgotten what I knew—that John was happy— and I hadn't lost my faith in a loving Savior. My pain did not supersede those things, but it was real nonetheless. I felt panicked—as though my foundation had just exploded and I was plunging down a dark shaft with no handholds. Eventually these feelings would pass and I would be centered once again in God's plan for me. But grief demands a toll on the road to recovery. I would have to pay its fee in full before coming out the other side. Thank heaven for loving family members who bore me up in my most vulnerable hours and for my children who gave me cause to keep going.

Later on, Kelly arrived and filled in more details about the rescue. He had spent all day out there searching, and as the afternoon wore on he became frustrated and tired. "I was worn out," he said. "We couldn't believe that he hadn't been found yet. But I couldn't give up. In a couple of hours the sun would go down and I didn't want to have to quit because of darkness. So I said a fervent prayer, Chris. Right there in the boat I silently promised the Lord that I would do everything I could to take care of you and the children if he would guide me to John. It was one of the most sincere prayers I've ever prayed and I had the feeling that Heavenly Father heard it. All day we had been taking our boat out a little farther than the buoys—just like you said, Chris—and after my prayer, we were out there ready to turn back north again, when we ran across something we knew was John, but he slipped away. We yelled for divers, but they were a long time in coming, and the wind was causing us to drift. We tried to set our hooks in the lake bottom to keep our position, but by the time the divers arrived, we were twenty or thirty feet off the mark. The two divers went down and it seemed they were under for a long time. But then, one came up and said that, yes, he was there, they had found him, and he asked us to call for backup."

"Did you help pull him out?" Lewis wanted to know.

"No." Kelly looked down at his hands. "I couldn't." Then he looked at me. "I ... didn't want to see him like that, Chris. Johnny and I were friends. I didn't want that image to cloud my memories of him. So I asked to be taken in, and I watched the rescue from shore. I stayed until they drove him away."

Then Kelly was silent.

John was pulled from Yuba Lake at 5:15 PM on Tuesday, April 28, 1987. He was found in twenty-two feet of water and had been under for over thirty-two hours. Involved in the search were over sixty people from the Juab and Millard County Search and Rescue teams, East and West Juab emergency medical technicians, Utah Highway Patrol, State Parks and Recreation, and Juab and Millard County Sheriff Departments. They were assisted by scores of volunteers from as far away as Salt Lake City. I would always be grateful for these dedicated men and women, friends and strangers. They brought my Johnny home when I could not. But I feel most grateful for Lewis, whose humble prayer united our hearts in petitioning the heavens for help, and for Kelly, whose faith made him an agent in the Lord's hands for answering that prayer. How blessed I felt to have this family. What light they lent to my darkest hours. I was a new widow, yes, but I was a daughter and sister, too. I learned that it is through these eternal roles that God so often bares his sustaining arm.

Eventually, Kelly and the others left, and Dad and Mom and I took the kids and went home. Dad helped me call the mortuary to make arrangements for the next day. Then we had dinner and put the children to bed. After Mom and Dad retired I checked on the children and found them all asleep. They had been real troopers these two difficult days. They must have been exhausted. I considered the source of their strength and realized that they were strong kids because they were John's kids. I was overcome with love and gratitude for them. It was through these children, I knew, that Johnny would live on.

Grief still burdened my soul, but John had been found, and I felt more at peace that night than I had since the accident. I got ready for bed, shut off the lights, and lay under the covers thinking about my husband. I remembered his happiness the morning we left for the lake. His enthusiasm had been boundless. I knew he would have taken his enthusiasm with him into the next world—it was one of his gifts. How I envied those who associated with him now. I realized that John had died doing what he loved best: enjoying the outdoors with his family. This idea gave me solace and some of the joy I had felt that morning returned to gladden my heart.

A moment later, my mind did something it hadn't been able to do the night before. It let go. My body followed, and I fell willingly into a deep and profound sleep.

Chapter Seven

$\mathcal{I}$ was awakened by Clint's cries. It was 7:00 AM. I went to his room, and when I picked him up, he calmed immediately. Cuddling him close, I thought, Clint, my dear one, you're just eighteen months old. Will you even remember your daddy?

My parents were up. They would leave soon for their own home, just blocks away, to shower and dress. Later they would return to tend the children while I went to the mortuary in Fillmore.

"How'd you sleep?" Mom asked when I went to the kitchen for Clint's bottle.

"Like a log," I answered, "all night long."

"Good," Dad said. "You have a big day today. The Monsens are coming to pick you up at 9:45."

"I'll be ready."

"You okay?" he said.

I sighed. "I'm not looking forward to this."

He put his hands on my shoulders. "Do you want us to come along?"

"No. I'll survive," I said, but I wasn't convinced. Making funeral arrangements, choosing a casket and headstone, writing an obituary, deciding on a burial place, maybe seeing John's body for the first time—these were loathsome, but unavoidable tasks. Completing each one would be like walking an emotional minefield and purposely setting off the mines one by one. I was in for many shocks to the heart today.

Mom put her arm around me. "Honey," she said, "our prayers are with you. It won't be easy, but remember, everything you do today will be for John. You'll be glad afterwards that you did them."

"I want to make everything perfect for him," I said.

"You will." She gave me a squeeze. "We'll be back soon."

I walked my parents to the door and watched them drive away. It was a crisp morning. The glow of the sun was spreading behind the Pavant Range to the east. John had loved those mountains. He would rather have been there than any other place on earth. He had explored every ridge and canyon—on foot as a boy, and on horseback as a man. I wondered if even now his spirit might be up there. How I wished I were just waiting for him to come home from the hills, as I had so many times before.

I closed the door and then woke up Melanie.

"Will you play with Clint for a while so I can shower?" I asked her.

"Okay, Mommy," she said, then sleepily carried him to the living room.

I headed for the bedroom, still thinking about John and the mountains. As I neared the end of the hall, I felt a warm sensation rise in my chest and radiate outward.

John was near.

I stopped in the doorway and felt an incredible joy flood my heart. John, you're here, I thought.

In answer, my husband's warm, resonant voice, entered my mind. "Yes, Chris," he said. "I wanted you to know something."

What is it? Tell me.

"Chris, there is a Christ. He was there to meet me when I died."

These words flowed like cool water through my soul.

"He knew me, and called me by name. He comforted me, encircling me with his love. He said, 'Thou good and faithful servant, thy work is well done.' He told me that I had accomplished everything Father in Heaven had assigned me on earth and that now I was needed here."

"Oh, Chris!" he continued. "He lives!"

I leaned against the door frame and closed my eyes. Tears streamed down my cheeks. I was not aware of anything except the beautiful cadence of John's comforting words. I felt weightless.

"I also met my brother Michael," John's voice continued. "He is a fine and noble being. And I saw my ancestors—all those who had gone before me. They knew me and I knew them. It was a joyous reunion."

I couldn't pinpoint where John was. He was inside of me and surrounding me all at once. It was a glorious, miraculous feeling. The meaning of his words sank deep into my understanding. He was communicating to me with more than just words. It was as if I had experienced for myself what he described.

He went on, "I also saw all the spirits of our posterity. I was overwhelmed with joy. Our posterity is greater than you could ever imagine, Chris. Our children's children, and their children, and their children, and on and on. They will accomplish marvelous works. You should be very proud.

"And Chris," now his words touched my innermost feelings, and I felt his love for me, "I went to the premortal world and met our baby's spirit. We spoke. What a strong and special spirit! This child will bring you happiness, Chris." And then I felt him leaving, his words and his presence slipping away. "Lots of happiness," he whispered and was gone.

John, don't go! I opened my heart to him and listened, trying to sense if he were still near. Oh, Johnny, I'm so happy when you're near. But he had left me. Now I was alone.

But his words still burned in my mind. I went to the bed and dropped to my knees. John had been met by the Savior! What sweet consolation to my soul. It was another witness that Christ does live. My Johnny had seen him, had been accepted and loved by him. Now I knew that if John had been terrorized at his death, or pained by leaving his family behind, his suffering would have been wiped away when he met the Lord. The Savior would have soothed him, given him peace and understanding. And knowing that the Lord had declared John's mission in life complete made me feel that my husband's reward was assured. I felt privileged to be his wife.

And I was *still his wife!* Though the veil divided us, our marriage had not ended. He continued loving me as I loved him. Death had changed many things, but some it had not.

I wanted to stay there on my knees forever, bathing in the glow of this beautiful experience. I preferred it to what faced me at the mortuary. What stark opposites were John's world and mine. Touching his world brought joy and light; returning to mine brought sadness and gloom. Regardless of what I now knew about John, I still must live without him, and my heart was rebelling. But I was thankful, *so thankful,* that John had come. It was a blessing beyond compare.

In a few moments I got up and went in for a shower. I relaxed and let John's words linger in my mind. His message that our unborn child was a special spirit sank deep into my heart. I already loved this tiny one—it's life still new since conception. I pressed my hand to my womb and wondered...was John's final purpose in life to engender this last child? Was his death delayed until all *six* of our children were here? I felt this was so.

After my shower I dressed and went back into the bathroom to do my hair. I had just started when I felt another impression of John.

"Chris," he said. "Go to the closet and look for a book from IPP." The Intermountain Power Project where

Johnny had worked. "Find the information concerning benefits for life insurance. Read it and understand it well. Then go and tell my dad."

He was very direct, as John could be when he wanted something done, so I quickly finished my hair and went to the closet. I found the book and opened it to the section Johnny had asked me to study. When I saw what was there, I became excited and surprised. The benefits listed for accidental death were not what I had expected at all. The day before, John's dad had asked me about insurance and I knew only that there would be money to cover funeral expenses. "Five thousand dollars," I had told him. But now I saw that the sum was much larger—enough that, if carefully invested, it would provide security for me while I raised my family, as well as money for missions and weddings for the children. Waves of relief swept over me—and amazement, and gratitude, and joy.

I ran back to the bathroom to put on my makeup so I could go tell John's dad. I was just putting on my mascara when John's voice returned.

"What are you doing?" he asked.

It's quite obvious, I'm doing my makeup, I thought.

"Quit primping and go tell my dad!" came his firm response.

All right, all right. I didn't know I couldn't do my face first!

Now I knew we take our personalities with us when we die, because this was just like Johnny. When he wanted something done, he wanted it done *now!* I put down the mascara, grabbed the insurance booklet, and obediently headed out the door for the Monsens'. At a run.

I found John's dad watching early morning TV.

"Chris!" he said. "Is everything all right?"

"Everything's fine, Dad." I was a little out of breath. "Listen. I need to tell you about something that just happened."

"Are the kids okay?"

"They're fine. What I need to tell you has to do with Johnny's insurance. Dad, he was just here, I mean his spirit came to me at home. Look." I opened the insurance booklet to the page that listed death benefits. "John told me where to find this book and which section to look up." I pointed to the page. "This shows the benefits I'll receive from John's life insurance policy."

Lewis read down the page. Tears filled his eyes and spilled down his cheeks.

"Chris, do you know what this means?" His voice was choked.

I nodded my head. "It's wonderful, isn't it?"

"It means you'll be able to stay home and take care of your family. You'll be okay. You don't know how I've worried. Since yesterday when you told me you'd be receiving only funeral benefits I've felt sick. I knew I couldn't support all of us on my schoolteacher's salary. I didn't know what to do."

He went on to tell me about his sleepless night, how he'd stayed up worrying and praying until dawn and then had driven to his little ranch, White Bush, to put out hay for the livestock. He had done the chores with a heavy heart, burdened with a sense of deep responsibility for me and the children. He had knelt down by a fence post and pled again with the Lord for an answer to his dilemma.

"And then the Lord answered my prayer," he continued. "I felt peace in my heart and was assured that everything would work out. It was made known to me that John was happy where he is—which is a great blessing—but I still didn't know how I would take care of us all. I figured I would just have to exercise my faith, you know. I came home and turned on the TV to try to relax."

"John must have known how you've worried," I said. "He wanted me to hurry over and tell you about this. He wouldn't even let me finish my makeup!" I laughed. "You know, a year ago when John started work at IPP we were glad for the opportunity, but I didn't know about these benefits. Where John worked before, the benefits were nowhere near this high. We've been really blessed."

"I'm so relieved, Chris," Lewis said, tears welling up in his eyes again. "You're going to be just fine."

We hugged and I felt a greater love for my father-in-law. Our relationship was changing with the death of his son. He felt more responsible for me and I felt more dependent on him. We would not grow apart with the death of his son; instead, we would grow closer.

"Thank you," I said.

"For what?"

"For everything."

"And thank *you*," he said. "You're doing so well, Chris. You are an example to the family."

"No, sometimes I don't even know how I'll make it from one minute to the next," I smiled. "But that's when the Lord steps in and sends me strength."

We parted and I went home to finish getting ready. The experience that morning made me realize that John was still involved in our family's affairs. He was near and would intervene whenever our greatest needs arose. The future was starting to look a little less bleak.

Later, John's parents picked me up and we headed for the Olpin Mortuary in Fillmore. Riding the ten miles along the highway, I thought how surprising it seemed that I should be going to a mortuary to arrange my own husband's funeral and burial. Everything was happening so quickly now that Johnny had been found. Of course *no one* has the chance to get used to these things, and I felt every bit the reluctant widow. And the closer we got to Fillmore the more reluctant I got. Slow down! I wanted to shout. Please, I'm not ready for this. Everything was too new. I couldn't get any perspective. How was I supposed to make important decisions at the mortuary with my erratic emotions? And they weren't pleasant decisions like, "John, I think we should marry in the Manti Temple, what do you think?" but instead, "John, where and in what shall we bury you?" I hated what I was going to have to do. It was like somebody holding John's death right in front of me and saying, "Look hard, Chris. This is real. Deal with it."

But my love for John was true. It was my one constant emotion. He was still alive—we had simply entered a new phase of our lives together—and like my mom had said, I was doing this for him.

I looked out the window and saw the sign, "Fillmore, 1 Mile," and tears fell from my eyes. "I'll do anything for you, Johnny," I whispered. "Even this."

Mr. Olpin, the owner and director of the mortuary came out to meet us when we arrived. He was middle-aged with dark hair and a gentle smile. He invited us in and expressed his sympathy to me and to John's parents.

Inside was a thickly carpeted foyer with cushioned chairs and small ornamental tables with lamps. The atmosphere was hushed. I stood there for a moment and an odd feeling came over me. John is supposed to be here, somewhere, I thought. They had told me he would be brought here after the medical examiners determined the cause of death. After searching for his body for so long, I wanted to make certain John was here, and I could think of no other way to be sure except to see him. Although I wasn't certain I could bear it, I asked Mr. Olpin if it would be possible to see my husband.

He didn't answer immediately, as if he was unsure of what to say. Then he said, "Mrs. Monsen, I think it might be better if you didn't see him this morning. They brought him in late last night and we haven't had time to get him ready."

"Please," I said. "I won't take long."

Mr. Olpin looked at Lewis and Janet and then back at me and said, "It really might be best if you wait. I'm sorry. But before I forget, Mrs. Monsen, I have something for you." He pulled John's watch out of the pocket of his black suit and handed it to me. "He was wearing this when they brought him in."

As I took the watch, a warm feeling flooded through me. Now I knew that John's body *was* here, and that was enough. I didn't have to see him.

And the watch was still running! All those hours in the lake and Johnny's watch had never stopped. It seemed to be a tiny manifestation that life goes on, that John himself lived on. And suddenly I knew by a feeling inside that John again was somewhere near. I felt comforted just by holding the watch tightly in my hand. The Lord sends us comfort sometimes by such small means.

We sat down and started planning the viewing, funeral, and burial. Janet and Lewis made suggestions and together we arranged services we thought John would approve of. The viewing would be at the mortuary that next evening, Thursday, and the funeral would be in the Holden Ward building on Friday, the first of May. We selected the music and speakers, and decided who would pray and dedicate the grave. Then we listed John's accomplishments for an obituary. He had achieved many good things during his twenty-nine years, and I felt proud of my husband.

Later, chills ran through me as we walked into a room filled with coffins of many different colors and designs. Was this for real? How do you *do* this, pick a casket for someone you love? I thought of one of the heavy lids closing over John's face. I shut my eyes and willed the image away.

We walked slowly, examining them; then one of the caskets caught my eye. It was a rich bronze—one of John's favorite colors. I went over to it and laid my hand on its smooth surface. It was cool to the touch. I could see my reflection in the satin finish. Mr. Olpin came over and lifted the lid. The lining of the lid was cream colored satin. In the center of the fabric was printed some stalks of wheat, the heads bent over with heavy grain, ready for the harvest. The inside of the casket was lined with the same creamy satin as the lid. It looked comfortable to lie in. I imagined my husband there, his eyes closed, his body stretched out the length of the casket. It seems strange, but I knew John would be happy there.

"I like this one," I said, and then more softly. "It reminds me of him."

Lewis and Janet came to my side.

"It's beautiful," said Janet.

Lewis nodded. His eyes were filled with tears.

"It *is* beautiful," Mr. Olpin said and after a moment closed the lid.

When we left the room we felt sad, yet strangely content.

Next, Mr. Olpin showed us a catalogue filled with headstone designs. "If we call in our order today," he said, "it will be ready for Memorial Day."

A headstone for John's grave, a visual beacon, something permanent in granite; it would mark the place I would honor him, feel near to him. In choosing it, as with choosing the casket, I was not making selections based solely on what John would like, but on what satisfied *me* as to what John would like. It was like choosing gifts for Johnny. I had to find what represented best my love for him.

We chose a polished, rust-colored granite stone embellished with oak leaves to represent John's love of the outdoors. It would have a place for John's full name, Lewis John Monsen, on the right and mine, Christine Tuttle Monsen, on the left—an etched image of the Manti temple would be in the middle to symbolize our eternal love. In an upper corner would be the round insignia of the Utah State Firemen's Association of which John had been a member. Across the bottom were to be engraved the names of our children, left to right, with room at the end for the sixth.

Mr. Olpin said, "And have you given thought to where he will be buried?"

"We have plots in the Holden Cemetery," Lewis said. "There's a place near our infant son's grave."

I knew the spot. It was near a spreading spruce tree high on the crest of the cemetery hill. It was a peaceful place with an impressive view of Holden, the rolling spring-fed hills beyond, the majestic mountains behind, and the Delta valley below. It was perfect. This was John's country. He was born to it, had roamed it countless times in life, and would lie at the heart of it in death until that bright day when trumpets sounded and he would rise again.

With the burial plot chosen, our purposes at the mortuary had come to an end. The final events in the mortal life of John Monsen were set into motion. I felt he was pleased with what we had decided, and I was satisfied too. And comforted. Mother was right, now that the business was done, I was glad to have done it. No one else on earth loved John as I did. It would have been wrong to have given over these responsibilities to someone else. As painful as it had been, making arrangements for John fulfilled and magnified my love for him. I felt I had proven I would do anything for him, make any sacrifice, walk through any fire.

I only hoped this same strength would see me through the many long days without him.

I was still holding John's watch. Now, as we left the mortuary, I tucked it into my purse. It was a precious token, one I would treasure the rest of my life. Mr. Olpin saw us to our car and we drove home.

Arriving in Holden, I wanted to go to bed and rest. The emotional strain of the trip to the mortuary had made me tired. But the next few days would be difficult for the family and I realized I needed to prepare the children for what was to come. In all my prayers I had prayed hardest for help with the kids. Now I would need to exercise faith that help would come. I gathered my courage and called my five children into the living room and we sat together on the couch.

"Where's Daddy?" Michael asked right off.

"He's with *Heavenly Father*," answered Stephanie in a tone that said he should know this already.

I jumped in. "Well, Daddy's spirit is with Heavenly Father, that's right, Stephanie. You already know what happens when someone dies. Their spirit leaves the body and goes to the spirit world, a beautiful place where they wait for the resurrection."

"That's where our daddy is," said four-year-old Jennifer.

"Yes," I said. "And he is very happy there. He's busy doing lots of things and learning lots of things. It's not a place where you just sit around."

Clint was getting restless so I held him on my lap. I knew he wasn't understanding any of this, but we all needed to be together for this talk.

Stephanie asked, "Is there any waterskiing in the spirit world?"

"No, Stephanie," Melanie answered. "There's no boats there."

"How do you know?" replied Stephanie. "Daddy could build one."

I laughed. "I think Daddy's too busy to waterski. Jesus has things for him to do, and he has to watch over us and make sure we're all okay."

Melanie asked, "Mommy, have you ever seen the spirit world?"

"No. I haven't seen it. But I know it's there. It's a perfect place—and all the spirits are peaceful there."

"Except the bad guys," said Stephanie.

"No, I imagine even the bad guys are peaceful. They're learning about their mistakes and are growing. Other people are teaching them who they are and how to change. Do you remember in the Bible? Even Jesus taught them after he died. Eventually, everyone will have a chance to choose what's right. Maybe Daddy is there, teaching people about Jesus. Or maybe he's helping get things ready for when Jesus comes again."

The children were quiet. John and I had taught them these things before, but they were understanding them now. Being able to picture their daddy there made it easier to imagine the life beyond. Children are so receptive to truth. They know it when they hear it.

"I just want you to know that whatever Daddy is doing, he is happy and he still loves you. He is still your daddy and nothing can change that, ever. Someday we'll be with him again and you'll see."

Now for the hard part, I thought.

"We need to talk about something else," I continued. "So I need you to listen carefully. When Daddy went to the spirit world, it was only his spirit that went. He left the earthly part of him, his body, behind."

"That's what they were looking for for so long in the lake," said Melanie. "But they couldn't find him."

"Yes, we were all worried, weren't we? It was important to find his body so that we could bury him properly."

"Uncle Kelly found Daddy's body," said Stephanie.

"Yes, he did."

"Where is it now?" she asked.

"In the funeral home—a place where they will take care of him and get him ready to be buried."

"Can we see him?" asked Melanie.

"Yes, in fact there's a special time when we will all go and see him together. It's called a viewing. It's tomorrow and all your cousins and aunts and uncles will come too." Everyone got excited about seeing all the cousins.

"What does he look like?" Melanie asked.

"He'll look like Daddy always looks, only his eyes will be closed like he's sleeping and he'll be very still. You won't even see him breathing because Daddy's alive in his spirit, not in his body."

"Can he hear us if we talk to him?" asked Stephanie.

"Daddy's spirit can. He can hear you from heaven and see you and at some special time he may talk to you, if you are listening carefully. But his body can't hear, or see, or talk. As long as Daddy's spirit is not inside of it, the body is not alive."

"Can we touch it?" Melanie wanted to know.

"If you want to," I said. "But the skin might feel cold."

Stephanie wrinkled her nose at that.

I continued. "Daddy's body will be lying in a casket, a beautiful long box with a lid. And when it's time for the burial, they will close the lid and lock it tight and then put the casket in the ground and cover it up with dirt. And there his body will stay safe until the resurrection. Do you know what that is?"

Everybody nodded, even three-year-old Michael, following his sisters' example.

"It's when Jesus will make Daddy's body brand new again and put his spirit back into it. Then he will be alive again forever! His body and his spirit will never be separated after that and Daddy..." I choked up with the beauty of these words: "Daddy will never die again. And it will be the same for each of you and for me. We'll all live again and we'll be with Dad forever if we do what's right and obey Heavenly Father's commandments."

The children had more questions and we stayed on the couch until late in the afternoon and every question was answered. I was pleased it had been so easy. I've learned that it's best to talk to children as if they were small adults—tell them plainly what they need to know and tell the truth. If you want the Spirit to help you talk with children, you must be straightforward and honest; the Spirit does not beat around the bush.

That night while putting them to bed, I sensed that each of my children would be fine, even though they would miss the love their father had lavished on them.

Little Clint was a bit fussy. These last few days must have seemed topsy-turvy to him; cared for by several different people, his schedule had been thrown to the wind. Michael had been the recipient of a lot of attention and had remained as energetic as ever. He was missing his dad, I could tell, but being so young I thought he might be the first to bounce back. Jennifer was an independent little girl. Sometimes it was hard to tell what she was thinking. Being the middle child, I hoped she didn't feel lost in the shuffle. I would try to show her as much love as the others during the days to come. Stephanie, too, would need my love. She understood enough to be frightened by what had happened. I would give her lots of assurance that she would be all right. And Melanie—my helper, my worrier. She would be the first of my children to go through real grief. Her emotions would feel strange to her, as mine did to me. She might need the most attention and love of all. But I sensed in her a great ability to shoulder this burden, and others that would come from being the oldest. In a way she would need to become the second parent of this incomplete family. I was grateful that God, in his wisdom, had sent such a capable spirit for the task.

One thing I knew for certain—all of my children would come to feel keenly the loss of their father as they grew older. They would grieve for him from time to time the rest of their lives. Since I could never replace John and be both father and mother, I committed myself to become the best mother I could to my children. I would soothe their pain when I was able, but I could not prevent it. Each one would have to come to terms with John's loss for themselves.

That night we all went to bed early. As the darkness of the night deepened, I lay there feeling the bleakness of a future without John. Having enough money to get by on was one thing, but having my husband is what I would have preferred. I was still shocked and confused and not at all ready to contemplate living alone. This was my third night without him. The empty place in my bed was like a dark, fallow field.

Johnny, you've left me, I cried in my heart. You're far from me in a place I can't get to. How I miss you, Johnny. *How I miss you . . .*

Chapter Eight

*C*hris, there's not much time left. You have to get ready,"
one of my sisters was saying. I thought it was Jill.

"Okay, okay, I know," but I continued to drag my
feet. The hour of the viewing was growing near, and I
didn't want it to arrive.

If I put off getting ready for it, I thought, maybe I can
postpone it.

"Chris, really. Is there something I can do to help?"
This time it was Tracie. She, Jill, Jayne, and Laurie—all of
my sisters—had come to help us get to the viewing.

"No, I'm doing fine. I'll be ready." But I didn't move.

It was downright irrational behavior. There I was, sitting on the edge of the bed in my slip, and time was growing
late. But I was in no hurry. I knew seeing John would break
my heart, and I had endured enough these last few days.

I didn't want to see him because I knew he would be
lying there stiff, and I wanted to see John alive, vibrant,

glowing with that special charm of his. I wanted him moving about, at a loss for something to do with his hands like I'd seen him a million times. I didn't want to see a blank, dormant face; I wanted his teasing grin, that tender gaze only I knew. I didn't want to be kept at arm's length by death's formality. I wanted to at least be granted that final farewell embrace of lovers we had been denied by so small and yet so deadly a thing as the temperature of water.

"Chris, I'm going to die," he had said. And then his last, verbal embrace: "I love you, Chris. We'll be together again."

Then he had slipped out of sight.

Until now. This viewing.

And I didn't want to go.

I knew the viewing would end in a few hours, and then after a brief night's sleep would come the funeral and the burial. Then it would all be over. Johnny would disappear again, this time for the rest of my life.

I wasn't ready. I needed more time.

And so I took it, getting ready for the viewing.

"Come on Chris, your kids are going to be ready before you are," This time it was Laurie pleading from the hall.

"John, do I have to do this?" I said quietly to the ceiling.

No response.

He was at the funeral home, I guessed, waiting for me there. He was probably wanting me to hurry up, too. Well maybe I'll stand him up this once, I thought. It would serve him right.

He had stood me up the day we were married. It was after the ceremony and the pictures had all been taken—John and I in front of the temple, John and I at the side of the temple, John and I walking towards the temple, John and I under the trees near the temple. It was a beautiful day, and the temple looked magnificent under the Manti sun, and so did John and I in tux and gown. The photographer had flown himself down from Springville. When he was all packed up he needed a ride back to the airport. Well, John had this love of flying and airports; he also had this zest for life that sometimes caused him to mix priorities. So he decided he would take the photographer to the airport in Ephraim himself.

"John, no," I said.

"It will only take fifteen minutes, tops," he said.

I couldn't believe he was really going. But I thought that maybe John felt responsible—the guy had come all this way for *our* wedding, after all. So I agreed to wait for him at the temple.

He and the photographer headed for the airport, and our families left to go to Gunnison for the wedding breakfast. I went back inside the temple to the waiting room—where I waited.

The governor of the state of Utah was flying into little Ephraim that morning. The airport was jammed with security people and the press. John got into the place but could not get out until the governor's plane had departed again. Fifteen minutes stretched into an hour, and I was getting concerned glances from the matrons in the temple. I was beginning to have concerns of my own. I could see

Johnny wanting to take the plane up for just a little spin, but I couldn't believe he would do it on our wedding day!

When he finally showed up I was a little perturbed until he told me what had happened. We ran to the car and headed for Gunnison.

At the restaurant everybody gave us a hard time. "*Where* have you two been?" they wanted to know. When I realized what they were implying I became embarrassed and made Johnny tell them the truth. He didn't want to at first, taking pleasure in prolonging the little joke.

What a wiseacre you were, John Monsen.

But he had been wonderful a few minutes later—my handsome new husband, standing at the head table, expressing his simple joy and telling of his love for each family member in turn. I had been so proud. And so much in love.

And here I am, avoiding you, Johnny. It's just that I can't bear to see you lying there. Lifeless.

After a moment, I thought how John had always insisted on being places on time. He'd gotten me up and out to many a meeting well before their appointed hours. If he were here, he'd be siding with my sisters.

I sighed and got off the bed.

Okay, John . . . you win.

There was a knock on the door. "Chris!" This time it was Jayne. Now I'd heard from all four.

"All right, all right. I'm coming!"

I quickly dressed in a white jacket over a polka-dot blouse and a dark skirt, then rode to the mortuary with my mom and dad. My children had gone over already with John's parents and were waiting outside when I arrived. Melanie, Stephanie, and Jennifer wore their matching yellow dresses I had made them for Easter. Michael and Clint wore matching blue shirts. They looked so sweet. If John was watching his family walk together up to the mortuary door, I know he was smiling.

Mr. Olpin met us inside. There were flower arrangements placed here and there and the lamps in the foyer were turned on, giving the room a warm glow. From somewhere, soft music played.

"Shall we go in?" Mr. Olpin asked.

I lifted my chin and met his eyes; his expression was so kind.

When we walked into the viewing room, I had to catch my breath. It was bursting with flowers! Magnificent, vibrant, radiant flowers. There were bouquets and wreaths and sprays of color everywhere, hanging on the walls, sitting in stands and arranged on tables, even resting on the floor. I had never seen so many flowers in one room in all my life. I realized that each one was a testament to John, to his life, and to how many people had known and loved him.

Then I let my eyes move to the center of the room, where, surrounded by blossoms, sat John's gleaming, bronze casket. The lid was open. And there lay John. I could see his head and his chest inside the coffin.

I felt a rush of blood to my face as my heart wrenched and began pounding wildly. Oh, John, I cried in my heart. I can't bear this. My beloved... how, in all the world, did this happen? I started toward him, and the children followed. Time seemed to slow as I walked. All other sights and sounds faded except the sight of my husband and the sound of my heart thrumming in my ears. My legs felt weak, and I thought I might fall. This was the moment, the agonizing moment I had tried to postpone: seeing and knowing again that my Johnny was truly gone.

I reached the casket and held onto it for support as the children gathered around me. A pall of sadness fell around me as I gazed down at his face. He was pale, and his hair was combed wrong, but everything else was in place—his clothing was sparkling white and crisply starched. A feeling of deep despair rose in my chest, grew, and spread into my limbs. In a moment I knew it would consume me, and I would start to sob. But then I heard Melanie crying softly, and realized my children needed me. This was a difficult moment for them, too. Somehow I garnered enough control to comfort them. I uttered soft words and touched each one, letting them know I was there.

"It's okay," I said over and over. "I love you. Remember what we talked about. Daddy is with Heavenly Father and he's happy. Everything's all right." Tears rolled down my face. "It's okay to be sad. Mommy's right here."

After a moment the children began asking questions. "Why is Dad's face so white?" "Can we see his legs and feet?" By now it was difficult to talk. My children's pain was harder for me to bear than my own. I found myself unable to answer their questions. I was afraid that if I let out another sound, it would be a wail of grief. I was grateful to let the grandparents take over.

I continued looking at John, studying his face through my tears. I laid my hand on his arm and a strong feeling of love for him came over me and mixed with all my despair. While we live, our bodies clothe our spirits and are beautiful creations in themselves. And Johnny was *beautiful* to me. I had loved his form, his broad shoulders, his muscular arms and sturdy legs. I had taken pleasure in his athletic abilities and had felt at home wrapped in his loving embrace. I knew every inch of him, knew the topography of his skin, the weight of each limb, the choreography of his movement, the cadence of his heart, the timbre of his voice. We had been as intimately entwined as the closest of husbands and wives; we had become one. And yet, standing there next to him, I felt the intractable expanse that divided us.

Or was he so far away?

He had come to me in spirit, hadn't he? Had caused me to feel awash with his presence. Had spoken words of comfort and wonder. Had lifted me halfway to heaven. These memories of his visits swelled my heart and a measure of my suffering was erased. I opened my spirit to his and found him near. He is watching me now, I thought, and he wants me to be strong for his family and friends. This was *his* night after all. I closed my eyes and said a prayer in my heart for courage and control. While I prayed, the pall of sadness loosened its grip. I felt strength return to my legs.

Behind me, people were already arriving. Judging from the flowers, there were bound to be crowds. I wanted so much to accept their sympathy without falling apart. I wiped my eyes, turned, and took my place at the head of the casket. Then I smiled and greeted John's first visitor of the evening.

It didn't take long before I realized that the night was *mine* too. So many friends came. Practically everyone I knew in Holden—which is practically everyone in Holden—showed up. Others came from Fillmore, Scipio, Meadow, and Kanosh. Every ward in our stake was represented. And others came from farther away. Though there were many sad farewells for Johnny, there were many joyful reunions for me. Even people I hadn't seen since my high school days in Springville came to let me know they still cared. I was surrounded all night by people who loved me. What a sweet and healing experience this was, to have so many others willingly share my burden. I didn't know how many good friends I had until I needed them and they came.

The viewing started at seven and was supposed to last two hours, but we weren't able to leave until after eleven.

Throughout the evening, Tracie, Jayne, Jill, and Laurie took good care of me, checking on me and bringing me a chair and little treats. Afterwards they helped gather the children and got us all out to the cars. A difficult evening was made lighter by their love for me.

Afterwards, I was exhausted. My feet ached and my mind was numb. Tracie came to spend the night. She helped me prepare a snack and put pajamas on the kids. Then we all went immediately to bed.

Lying in the darkness, scenes from the viewing played in my mind. The bright flowers. All the wonderful people. My children subdued at first and then getting impatient and a bit rambunctious as the evening wore on. Aunts and uncles taking charge of my kids. Melanie bursting into tears more than once.

I thought about how I had felt upon seeing John and I realized how the viewing had changed my feelings. Before, I had been reluctant to see him. But as the evening progressed I had grown almost used to him lying there, not moving, not breathing. I knew this wasn't John; it was just his most intimate and personal possession. And it seemed to represent the real Johnny the same way a statue commemorates someone's life. But it was not stony or unnatural like a statue. It was flesh and bones, *his* flesh and bones, and it was the closest thing on earth now to John himself. I had begun to feel comforted being near it. It brought me nearer to him.

The next morning I woke feeling lonesome for John. It was just as Carly Simon described in her song: "The wee small hours of the morning" *would be* the time I'd miss him most of all. But it was an emotion I let myself indulge in—today was his funeral and burial. Besides, I knew these feelings would be with me for a while. I was learning to relax and let them happen. I was even coming to trust them, knowing by experience now that they would not destroy me. Fearing them or fighting them only heightened my anxiety. By accepting them and giving in, the worst often passed sooner, and I felt better afterwards. A good cry does wonders when you need one.

"Are you okay?" Tracie asked when she saw me in the hall.

"Just missing John this morning," I said. "I'll be fine. I just want to get ready quickly and go over to the church. If I'm there first, I figure I can have some time with him alone. Can you bring the kids later?"

"Of course. They're awake; let's get them dressed."

When the children were ready, I left them with Laurie and drove over to the church. Unlike the night before, I was now in a hurry to see John. My remaining time with him was so short.

When I walked into the church, John wasn't there. I checked everywhere and couldn't find him. "Heavenly Father," I prayed. "Please bring John. I want to spend some time with him before everyone comes."

Mr. Olpin came through the door shortly. Two men followed him, pushing John's casket. They rolled it into the empty cultural hall. I waited until they left and then went in.

I walked up to the casket. The lid had been raised. I looked at John and saw that they had put more makeup on him. His face didn't appear so white. Other than that, he looked exactly as he had the night before. I thought about fixing his hair but was afraid it might look worse if I tried to change it now. I realized I only had a few minutes before Mr. Olpin returned with his helpers, so I leaned against the casket to get as close to John as I could and spoke softly to him.

"John," I said, "I will always love you more than you'll ever know. Please be happy. I will miss you."

My words seemed to resonate for a moment before evaporating into the cool air of the hall. The morning sun poured in shafts through the high windows and pooled on the shiny floor. The large room was bathed in a golden light. I exercised my faith that Johnny would hear me.

"I promise you," I continued with tears falling down my cheeks, "to do everything I can to be with you again. We are eternal partners, John. Though we've only been together for eight years in this life, we will be together forever in the next. I'll come to you, John. I promise it. I'll look forward with all my heart to that day when I'll see you again."

I stopped speaking and a sublime feeling flooded over me. I knew John had heard my words and I listened for an answer. One came.

"Chris," I heard John say. "I love you, too. And I am proud of you. Stay close to the Savior and to his gospel and you will receive comfort and be guided through the rough times. And Chris, I will be here for you . . ."

The lights came on and Mr. Olpin walked in.

I felt John's words fade, but they had been etched in my heart.

"Good morning, Mrs. Monsen. How are you doing?"

I tried to smile. "I'm doing all right."

"You're doing wonderfully," he said. "I hope everything turns out today just like you want."

"I'm sure it will," I said.

"Will you let me know if there's anything I can do?"

"Yes. Thank you."

He said something about bringing in more flowers and left.

By now some of the family members had begun to arrive, so I didn't get another chance alone with John. But I had been comforted immensely already and felt that my purpose for having come early had been accomplished. I continued to stand near him. I knew that his spirit was close by and this made me happy, maybe even a little giddy for a moment. I thought about rubbing in his makeup with my finger—it was a little caked in areas—but I didn't dare.

Kelly and his wife, Denise, had arrived and were positioning a large photo near the casket. It was of John and me and our five children. We'd had it taken only two days before John's death. Kelly had it enlarged and mounted. I went over to get a closer look. This final picture of us all would become our most treasured photograph.

Someone tapped me on the shoulder and I turned around.

"Bramwell!" It was John Bramwell, a missionary companion of Johnny's from the Minnesota Minneapolis Mission. John had always called him Bramwell and so had I. We hugged.

"Hi, Chris. I'm so sorry. You know how much I'm going to miss John."

"I know. That makes two of us."

We stepped over to the casket together and stood for a moment in silence.

"Bramwell, it's so good to see you." I said. "John would be happy you came."

John Bramwell and my husband were best friends. The two shared a bond that rarely exists between men.

They understood each other, had the same goals and dreams, and had enjoyed countless wonderful and crazy times together. I don't suppose there would have been any other man, besides family, that John would have been happier to be with. Normally, they would have greeted one another with hugs and slaps on the back.

But not today.

I could see in Bramwell's face how much he would miss his great friend. Johnny had worked his way deep into Bramwell's heart. And I knew it had been the same for Johnny. Nothing would have parted these two except death.

He held his hand out and I saw he had brought a little gift for John. It was a tie tack.

"It's beautiful," I said and picked it up. It was a tiny, golden Angel Moroni blowing his trumpet.

"May I do the honors?" he asked.

I nodded my head and handed it back to him.

Bramwell leaned down and lovingly attached it to John's white tie. It gleamed there, a token of love and remembrance between eternal friends.

Then Bramwell took John's hand in his. "We'll be buddies forever," he said.

In that moment I felt that John's spirit was thrilled with Bramwell's gift. I almost thought Johnny's buttons would pop off he was so pleased to be wearing that tie tack. I expect to see it there on resurrection morning.

Bramwell gave me another hug and left the hall. By now, there was a line of people waiting to see John. I was surprised so many had come for this viewing before the funeral. All of John's friends and co-workers at IPP were there. I thought everyone we knew had come the night before! But I was wrong. Even I had underestimated the widespread impact of John's life.

As they came through the line, so many people mentioned things John had done for them or taught them by his example. John had lived in Holden much of his life and through his service and his bright personality had won the hearts of people in the Church and community.

Holden was established by Mormon pioneers in 1855, and greeting its residents that morning, I sensed their pioneer strength, perseverance, and abiding love of God—qualities John had embodied. The town was named after Elijah Holden who perished in a storm on Scipio Pass while attempting to save a small boy's life—something John would have done. No wonder the townspeople felt he had belonged to them.

I remembered countless nights when John would come home, eat dinner, and leave again for five or six hours to lend someone a hand. John could fix anything and was a first-rate electrician. Many struggling farmers turned to him because they had no other way to get electrical work done or equipment repaired. John would tell them not to worry about paying him.

And John never missed home teaching or an elders quorum assignment. He was in the quorum presidency and often visited families besides those assigned to him, many of whom he was helping get ready for the temple. Later, they would come to me when they had their recommends and attribute the changes in their lives to John.

The night before he died, John gave a blessing to a sick boy in the ward. He blessed and held the child, and the boy got better.

John had a winning way with everyone. He loved to joke around and tease. He used this quality to work his way easily into people's lives. Thus, in times of need, they turned to him, and he was there. When he spoke, people listened. And when he bore his testimony, they were moved.

John had his weaknesses of course. Among other things, he got easily irritated when things weren't just right, and sometimes he was impatient with others who didn't live up to his expectations. He wasn't perfect. But while he lived, John used his endless energy and abilities to do many near-perfect things. And he had touched many lives in the process.

The time had come to start the funeral, but there were still so many people in line. We couldn't turn them away. We let the viewing continue until everyone who wanted to had come through.

Finally, when the line ended, Mr. Olpin asked the family to gather around. It was time for the family prayer. Overwhelming sorrow enveloped us, knowing that our time with John was at an end. During the prayer, so sweetly spoken by John's brother Gary, the Spirit entered our hearts bringing love and comfort. It manifested to us that this man we mourned had lived a good life, that his life had been cut short for a grand purpose, and that he would have his eternal reward.

After the prayer everyone said their final good-byes to John. Lastly, his dad leaned down and spoke some final quiet words to his son, and then the children and I gathered to John's side. I helped each one say a simple good-bye to him, then I gave John a last kiss on his forehead. We stood back while Mr. Olpin came forward to close the casket. With tears streaming down my cheeks, my handkerchief to my mouth, I gazed lovingly at my husband's face, taking advantage of every last second he was in view. Then the lid was lowered all the way and I could see him no more. With a final click, it settled into place, and Mr. Olpin engaged the lock.

The funeral was beautiful. John's brother Robert and Kelly gave loving and spirit-filled tributes to John. I cried many silent tears but not until the final musical number did I break down and weep. It was "The Circle of Our Love," sung by my brother Ken and his wife Lori. Johnny loved *Saturday's Warrior*—I guess because he felt he *was* one—and the words to this song expressed perfectly how we felt about each other.

"The circle of our love begins with now and every promised dream," Ken and Lori sang. "In God's eternal plan, it goes forever."

I felt John speaking to me through my feelings. Somewhere he was there, watching and listening, and was happy.

They continued, "The circle of our love, it stands beyond the reach of time, beyond the span of days and years, it goes forever.... that lips may breathe or hearts may beat forever."

Now, his spirit was near, telling me again how much he loved me and asking me to take care of his children.

In my heart, I answered him: *I will John. I love you and miss you. The circle of our love will go on forever.*

After the song ended, the room was filled with sniffles during the silence before the closing prayer.

At the cemetery the family was surrounded by crowds of people. It was a crystal clear day for the gathering at the crest of the hill. It was May Day; the grass was green and the air was fresh. It seemed Mother Earth had created a perfect day for receiving to herself a choice son.

During the dedicatory prayer, I drew my children close. This had been an emotional and confusing time for them. They were losing their dad, everyone around them had been crying for days, and the viewings and funeral had surely seemed strange to them. They were sad and frightened. I tried to comfort them with my touch, to let them know that everything would be okay. Their mother would not be leaving them.

John's brother Bryce completed the moving priesthood ordinance, and I clutched my children tightly as John's casket was lowered into the ground. At the sight of it sinking out of sight, abject loneliness fell upon my heart. I was desolate.

My parents helped me and the children to the car and drove us back to the church for a meal with family and friends.

After I ate, I found Bramwell and we had a long talk. I explained how John had died and about his rescue from the lake.

"Chris, this has been quite an ordeal for you," he said. "Are you going to be okay?"

"No," I answered. "And yes. Right now my emotions are in a turmoil, but I know I'll get better."

"It's going to take a long time," he said. "But that's okay. John is worth it." He smiled.

I found it so easy to talk to Bramwell. He had been at the temple when John and I were married. When we lived in Provo, John and I had often gone out with Bramwell and his wife, Suzanne, and he had visited us often at our apartment. I felt comfortable telling him things that I would not have told my parents or John's parents or anyone in the family—things that might have caused them pain, or worry. Families are important in this life; God ordained them. But I believe God ordained friendship, too. Friends provide a special kind of comfort and freedom that families can't.

I told Bramwell exactly how bad I felt, entrusting to him my tears and my pain. I needed a witness to the worst of my torment, someone who could say, "Yes, I understand those feelings and they are appropriate. Don't worry, Chris." Though Bramwell didn't say these words, his willingness to listen had the same effect.

And how well he had known Johnny! I loved reminiscing with Bramwell about John.

"Do you remember the time he hit his head at the racquetball court and forgot who he was?" Bramwell said.

"Yes. When you guys brought him home I just knew he was faking it. Johnny was always pulling pranks," I said.

"But it was real! It knocked him cold and when he came to, he didn't know where he was."

"I know it," I laughed. "He couldn't remember who I was either. I had to keep reminding him, 'I'm Chris, your wife,' and he'd say 'Oh, yeah.' But I knew he wasn't faking because later that night he asked me why his rifle was sitting behind the door. He had spent the night before cleaning it—the deer hunt was the next day. And there was also a tire in the living room for the truck to take the horses up the mountain. He asked about that too. Can you imagine Johnny forgetting about the deer hunt?"

"No way!" Bramwell laughed.

"And I didn't want him to go because I knew he'd forget where he was and get lost up there. His short-term memory was just gone for about three weeks."

"And wasn't it during mid-terms?"

"Yes. *That* was a real problem. He couldn't pass his tests because he couldn't remember what he had studied!"

Bramwell and I talked and talked and had some good laughs. I like to think Johnny joined in. It felt so good to laugh again.

Our friend Bramwell taught me that laughter and fond memories do a lot to chase the worst feelings away. I knew I would eventually heal, though I would never forget. And I would learn that life *does* continue after grievous loss. Joy *does* return.

Later that day the phone rang at home. I picked it up.

"Hello, Chris. It's Dave Larsen." One of the guys in John's shift at work. He and the rest of the crew had been off the same four days as John and because of the funeral, they were just getting back to work.

"Hi, Dave," I said, wondering why he was calling.

"Chris, the guys and I just got in to start the shift. And . . . there's something here we thought you ought to know about."

"There is?"

"Yeah," his voice was a little unsteady. "We got in here to the lockers to change and . . . our shoelaces were all tied together in knots."

I thought, why is he telling me this? And then I knew. *Johnny.*

"John did it, Chris," he said. "He was the last one to leave last week. And you know how he was always trying to get in the last good one on us? Well, he did it this time. He got the last laugh."

I couldn't say anything.

"He got us real good, Chris. You should see these knots. The guys are crackin' up."

I imagined I could hear John's friends saying, "Oh, that Johnny! That Monsen!" with tears coming to their eyes.

"We're gonna miss him down here, Chris," Dave said. "Just wanted you to know. He was the best."

"Yes. He was," I said. "The best . . ."

"Well, sorry to bother you," he said.

"Oh, Dave. No! Thanks so much for telling me. It really means a lot."

We said good-bye, I hung up the phone, and sat down. A mixed tide of sadness and joy flowed through me. I didn't know if in some sense Johnny had known he was saying good-bye to his friends at work. But I knew that by tying those knots he had been saying hello to life. It was his way. He had left behind a reminder of his endless zest for living.

Thinking of John this way brought an image of him to mind. It was early on the morning he died. I had watched him head off in a run along the path leading to his parents' home to get the boat. He had been luminous in the morning light. He was healthy and bursting with life. I watched him run across the field and it seemed as though his feet never touched the ground.

Over time, images like this would replace my memories of John lying lifeless in his casket. Like Kelly, who asked to be taken ashore when John's body was pulled from the lake, I would always prefer to remember John vibrant and alive—as I know he still is, on the other side of the veil.

I would also learn in the coming months, that my connection with John had not ended at the grave. We were still husband and wife, and our love would transcend boundaries in ways I could never have imagined.

Chapter Nine

*S*ister Monsen!" Sister Stephenson was calling me from across the foyer. It was the Sunday after John's funeral and I was on my way to teach the Mia Maids. I had brought the family to church in spite of our tragedy. I thought that sticking to our routine was important for the children. Besides, I knew how John felt about missing church. He would want us there.

"Sister Monsen."

I waited for Sister Stephenson to catch up.

"There's something I have to share with you," she said. "Do you have just a minute?"

I said that I was on my way to teach a class, but she assured me that this was important and would take only a minute. Sister Stephenson was one of the stalwarts of the ward. She and her husband were retired and lived just a few blocks from our home. I had admired and respected their faithful examples. "All right," I said.

We went into a quiet corner and Sister Stephenson said, "Chris, I had a wonderful experience in the temple last Tuesday, and I just couldn't wait to tell you. You know my husband and I are temple workers at the Manti Temple."

I nodded.

"On Tuesday, I was assigned to the celestial room, to tidy up and help the patrons if they needed anything."

She put her hand on my arm and lowered her voice to almost a whisper.

"A session was just ready to come through, and the workers were on their way to the veil, when I suddenly felt I should look towards the entrance of the room. And there was your husband, Chris. I saw John. In the celestial room."

"You did?" I said and felt a warmth in my heart that told me what she said was true.

"I did," she continued. Her face was serene as she spoke. "He was wearing a white suit. As he walked across the room, he turned and smiled at me and then went with the workers to the veil."

"He went with the workers?" I asked.

"Yes, he didn't say anything or do anything more than smile at me and disappear through the doorway. I saw him for just a moment, but I knew it was him. The way he turned to acknowledge me, I know he wanted me to see him and recognize him."

"Oh, Sister Stephenson. That's wonderful," I said. Tears spilled onto my cheeks. "How did he look?"

"Just the same. I knew him instantly. And of course we had heard the tragic news the day before, so I knew he had passed away. I was surprised to see him, but I wasn't shocked or afraid. He looked so calm and happy. His smile was his same famous smile."

"About what time did you see him?" I asked.

"It was the first session after lunch—I'd say around two."

Johnny had not been found by then. His body was still in the lake.

"On Tuesday?"

"Yes. It's such a beautiful testimony that our loved ones are happy and busy where they are. I wanted to tell you earlier in the week, but felt I should wait."

I pulled a hanky out of my purse—I had quite a supply in there—and wiped my tears. "Do you know," I said, "that on Monday morning Johnny and I decided we were going to go to the temple on Tuesday."

"Well, he was *there*." She smiled and nodded her head reassuringly.

I thanked Sister Stephenson for sharing. We hugged and I went on to my class.

All through my lesson and for the rest of the day, her words burned in my heart. I believed her experience showed that commitments made on earth can be kept on the other side of the veil. The temple is where John had determined to be on Tuesday, and that's where he was. Of course. John would be faithful to *all* his commitments. He would be fulfilling his new mission, and qualifying himself for the highest kingdom of glory. And he would be expecting me to join him there as his eternal companion. Now I had to follow through with *my* commitment to get there. Losing my place with John in the eternities would be more tragic, by far, than losing him momentarily by death. I would need to become a better person, live the gospel of Jesus Christ more fully, pray more regularly. I would need to spend more time studying scriptures and serving my neighbors.

These thoughts were reinforced by a letter John Bramwell had sent me after the funeral. He had written: "Chris, you and John did, do now, and will yet glorify each other." How I wanted those words to be true! But I felt so weak. John had always been the strong one. I had come to depend so much on his spiritual strength; I wasn't sure I could do it on my own. That Sunday night I dropped to my knees, and in fervent prayer, I told my Father in Heaven of my weaknesses and of my great need to overcome them. I pleaded for his help and placed myself in his hands. I prayed the same prayer again the next day and the next. Day after day I went to him in prayer, asking him to help me to change and to grow, to become the eternal companion John needed. I asked for the Spirit to lift me up, to help me through my grief, and to look forward, not back.

I began to study the gospel in earnest, in particular the plan of salvation as it pertains to life and death. I needed to know everything there was to know about John—where he was, what he might be doing, in what ways he would continue progressing. I wanted to know what the spirit world is like, how death figures into the eternal scheme of things. I knew the basics, but I wanted to know everything. I read every book I could find on these subjects, but most of my answers came from the scriptures.

Oh, the scriptures! What a huge source of comfort and inspiration they became for me. Many times while studying the scriptures, the Spirit consoled me and taught me things about life and the eternities I had never considered.

As for getting along without John, I took it one day at a time. For days and weeks following the funeral I was almost paralyzed from missing him. But I tried to stay busy, to keep myself moving. I refused to collapse into an immobile, mournful heap. Besides, I was pregnant. I had to stay active, positive, and healthy for myself and for the baby.

Melanie and Stephanie continued in school, and I settled back into a routine at home with Jennifer, Michael, and Clint. Though my extended family helped tremendously with the children, especially at first, I tried to spend extra time with each of my kids, focusing on their needs and trying to ease the burden of their father's death.

But sometimes it was difficult having strength enough for them—I was struggling under my own needs and burdens. As time went on and help from others waned, the demands of caring for my children often over-whelmed me. Feeding them, keeping them in clean clothes, getting them to bed at night and up in the morn-ing, cleaning up after them, keeping the little ones enter-tained and the older ones busy, responding to their demands: these were all parts of parenting I knew and accepted. But now I was doing them all alone, and I often found myself at the edge of exhaustion. Other aspects of parenting—teaching, training, correcting, disciplining—weighed heavily too. For, even though mine were good children, they *were* children, and I didn't have Johnny's strength and good judgment to back me up anymore.

And how I grieved for John! Some days I was enshrouded in a fog of sorrow and pain. Other days I was so numb I felt I barely existed. Living with the man you love is a habit hard to break. I quickly learned, however, that grief is not an illness, but a physician. By letting myself grieve appropriately, my capacity for life was returning.

The scriptures were helpful here, too. In them I regularly found solace and gentle, healing prescriptions for my suffering and strength for my daily challenges.

One scripture in particular worked miracles on a lonely night when I thought I couldn't survive another day without John. I had been packing up some of his things. I was surprised and shaken at the agony caused by simply folding a shirt and putting it into a box. When night came and the house grew quiet, my sorrow and loneliness only intensified. Sometimes when this happened I was able to pray and feel John near me, and tonight I really needed that blessing. But he wasn't there. In desperation I took the scriptures in hand hoping to find something there to ease my pain. I put my thumbs on the edge of the book and opened it by chance to Colossians, chapter two. This chapter contains Paul's words to the Colossians, but when I read them, they came as Johnny's words to me. Beginning with verse five, I read:

> *For though I be absent in the flesh, yet am I with you in the spirit, joying and beholding your order, and the stedfastness of your faith in Christ.*
>
> *As ye have therefore received Christ Jesus the Lord, so walk ye in him:*
>
> *Rooted and built up in him, and stablished in the faith, as ye have been taught, abounding therein with thanksgiving.*

The Spirit surged through me and joy melted my pain away. Johnny could not be with me in the flesh, *yet he was with me in spirit* and was watching over me. Here was healing balm in words I could turn to again and again whenever I needed reminding.

And yet the scripture bore another message—an injunction to walk in the way of Christ Jesus and be rooted in him. I needed this reminder. I saw that I had depended too much on a spiritual connection with John and not enough on the most important connection of all—my own with the Savior. There was no other name under heaven *but His* whereby I might be saved. If, through this scripture, John was pointing the way for me, it was in a direction away from himself and toward the Lord of all, the Good Shepherd, the Redeemer of the World.

I took this instruction to heart and as the days passed I felt my perspective shifting. Though I felt John nearby on occasion, I came to depend more fully on the Lord. Every week in church I was reminded that by keeping the Lord's commandments, I might always have his Spirit to be with me. And *this* is the blessing I sought.

Six weeks after John's death I woke one Sunday morning to the sound of the alarm. "Oh, no," I groaned. "It's here."

It was June 14th. Father's Day.

In church that day, there would be a special program dedicated to fathers. There would be talks about honoring fathers and all the children of the ward would stand up in front and sing songs they had practiced for their dads. How would my children take it? I wondered. How would *I* take it? I steeled myself then woke the kids.

"It's Father's Day today," said Melanie as she got up.

"It's Father's Day!" Stephanie echoed and ran into the boys' room. "It's Father's Day!"

So much for hoping they'd forget, I thought. It's too bad somebody's not sick so we'd have a good excuse to stay home. I went in to get the baby.

Soon all the kids were milling around me.

"We need to sing really loud," Melanie was telling the rest of them, "so Dad will hear us."

"We'll sing the loudest!" cried Stephanie.

"I know he'll hear us, Mom," said Melanie. "If we sing loud he'll be there to hear us."

Michael came to me and said, "Mom, will Daddy really be at church to hear me sing?"

"Your daddy loves you very much," I said. "And I know that he will want to be there."

"But Melanie says he *will* be!"

"Yes, Michael, if you really want him to hear you sing, I believe his spirit will hear you sing. If he does, you'll feel warm inside and that's how you'll know he heard."

"Oh, then I'm going to sing my loudest!" he said.

"Me too!" Jennifer added, and they ran to get dressed.

I hoped I had said the right thing, but I didn't have the heart to say anything else. Besides, I believed John *would* be there. The John I knew would be the last person on earth—or in heaven—to let his kids down.

At church I watched my children walk to the front with the other kids to sing. I could see their excitement. They beamed with as much pride as the others who had dads in the audience. As the children started to sing I kept an eye on Michael. He was standing in front with the littlest ones and had to stand on tiptoe to see over the little wall separating the podium from the congregation. His eyes sparkled and I saw by his effort that he was singing his best for his dad. Tears came to my eyes and a sob rose from my throat.

Oh, Johnny, I thought, these are precious little ones we have. Then my insides began to glow with warmth and joy, and I knew John was there and was hearing his children sing to him.

The second song began, "I'm so glad when daddy comes home, Glad as I can be. . ." The children did all the actions—clapping, tapping their knees, hugging themselves tight—then, "Pat his cheeks and give him what?" Michael puckered up. "A great big kiss." Smack!

The congregation chuckled and the kids squirmed with glee. Then the next song began. The chorus nearly did me in.

Fathers are so special
with a very special love.
They watch us and protect us.
They guide us and direct us
Back to our home above.

If spirits cry, then I knew tears were falling from Johnny's eyes.

Afterwards, Michael came running. "Mommy," he said, "my tummy feels warm. Daddy heard me sing!"

A few weeks later, it was time for another monthly visit to Dr. Jackson's office. This would be my fourth, and I wasn't looking forward to it. Prenatal exams are always unpleasant, but I was feeling especially reluctant to go. Though everything had checked out okay on my previous visits, lately I'd felt a little discomfort. I didn't want to learn that something was wrong.

"Hello, Chris," Dr. Jackson said warmly when he entered the examination room. "How are you?"

"Missing my husband," I said. "He's supposed to be here for this, you know." John had been actively involved in all my other pregnancies, following the progress, going with me to the doctor's to hear the heartbeat, to see the sonograms, and of course, he had always been there at the births of our children. "I guess he thought he could skip out on me for this one," I added.

"Well, maybe it was too much for him," Dr. Jackson said, picking up on my sarcasm. "He passed out on us once, remember?"

"Yes. That was with Michael. He was so excited to finally have a boy that he went crazy!"

"Right there in my delivery room."

When the doctor had announced it was a boy, Johnny was so ecstatic that he had launched into this little dance, whooping and hollering, spinning around and jumping up and down. Then he turned pale and slumped against the wall. The next moment he went limp and fell in a pile on the floor. He was out cold! Dr. Jackson with Michael in his arms—a big ten-pound boy—turned and looked at Johnny and said, "I think he got a little too excited. Leave him there—we'll take care of him in a minute."

"That was so funny!" I said. Not that I was laughing at the time. Michael was a *big* baby—it seemed I'd been in labor for days. But John was so happy to have a boy.

The doctor put his stethoscope in his ears and pressed the end of it against my stomach. He explored with the stethoscope until he found the right place, then listened for a minute. "It's fast. Chris, I'm calling it a girl."

This was no surprise. I had been expecting it to be a girl all along. I had already bought one little pink outfit. It was still early for shopping, but I was excited to have this child—John's final gift to me. He had spoken with the baby's spirit and had told me how special it was. I couldn't wait until it was born! I wanted to see it and hold it and know that it had been with him. It seemed the circle would then be complete. I would have a connection with John's spirit—in the flesh. The baby would be a constant reminder that eternity is real.

Later in his examination the doctor said, "Well, I think I know why you've had some discomfort. This baby is transverse, Chris."

This was unwelcome news. It meant the baby was lying sideways in the womb. A similiar problem had plagued me when I was carrying Clint. I knew from experience that as the baby grew, so would my discomfort and the probability of a C-section—I didn't want that again. Especially with *this* baby. When I had complained about not having John with me during this pregnancy, I was not kidding. I was not happy about going through this alone. Especially if there were going to be complications.

"But the good news is," the doctor continued, "the baby is healthy and growing well. I think everything will be fine, Chris. We'll monitor you closely. You have nothing to worry about."

Later, these words rang hollow as I left the office. Of course I have something to worry about, I thought. I'm a single mother of five young children and now a sixth is on the way with complications. This will certainly be a year to remember.

I wasn't feeling bitter, just sorry for myself and lonely. Tears sprang from my eyes and with all my heart I wished John were there.

As time went on my pregnancy did get more difficult. Carrying the baby sideways put extra stress on the muscles that supported my womb and it made my back ache. But somehow it was suddenly autumn, the kids started school again, and I realized I had made it through the summer.

By this time my friend Lorna had become an increasingly important part of my life. She was always there for me, whatever my need, and we developed the habit of talking every night on the phone. With her, like with Bramwell, I felt able to lower all my barriers and say the things I truly felt without fear of being misunderstood. Sometimes when I needed an outlet for my emotions, Lorna would come and let me talk until I could talk no more, cry until I could cry no more. She let me express fully what losing John meant to me, in whatever form that expression took—anger, regret, sadness, anxiety, fear—I was even able to joke with her about Johnny's death. Her loving, nonjudgmental ways were exactly what I needed in those early months of grief.

In those months the children and I talked many times about John's death, too. They were still curious about why he had died and how. In coping with their own grief, they wanted to talk again and again about their dad, his death and his life. I never turned them away from these subjects, and I always gave them the best answers I could.

At family get togethers the conversation would invariably gravitate to John. His brothers loved to reminisce about their many hunting adventures with him, and his parents enjoyed relating stories about his youth. I saw that everyone was dealing in his or her own way with the loss. Sometimes we shared our sorrow and were comforted by one another. It was good to be with others who had loved John and missed him as I did.

One night, I sat with John's mother in her kitchen, and we spoke of our loneliness for him. We mentioned all the things surrounding John's death that seemed to show that his death was meant to be—the wind and waves that pushed the boat out and then became suddenly still when he died, the life jackets that were left inside the boat, and the missing mooring line, which I had one day discovered with the gear for the horses. There was the last family photo we had taken the Saturday before. It seemed there were a lot of things that John had finished up before going or things that expressed a curious good-bye—like tying the knots in his co-workers' shoes.

I asked Janet, "Did I tell you about John's last talk with the children?"

"No, tell me," she said.

"It was on Sunday, two weeks before he died. The kids had been noisy in church that day, and when we got home, John called them all into the living room and sat them on the couch. Then he gave them a good talking to. He was a little upset at first, but then he calmed down and got really serious, and he said some meaningful things to them."

"What did he say?"

"He told them that they needed to try harder to obey. That obeying their parents was really important, especially obeying me. He told them how much he loved me and how they should love me too. Listening to their mother, he said, would bring them happiness, and honoring her would bring them eternal blessings."

"Did he put all the emphasis on you?"

"Yeah . . . and he had been in church that day too, trying to keep the kids quiet, but during this talk it was almost as if he knew he wasn't going to be raising them himself. He told them to obey me in public and in private, and to always show me lots of respect."

"It sounds as if he was giving his final instructions to them," Janet said.

I nodded. "And the kids just sat there. I could tell they were listening, so much more intently than usual. In the end he told them how much he loved them and wanted only the best for them."

"Johnny was a wonderful father," she said.

"Yes, he was."

"You know," said Janet, "we feel we had an opportunity to say good-bye to John. We've thought a lot about this and believe it's true."

"When was that?" I asked.

"On Sunday, the night before he died. He came over to the house for a short visit, and before he left, we all hugged. His dad put his arms around him and expressed his love for him. I did the same. We talked about the Savior and felt the Spirit. We didn't understand why we were having such a loving experience. Now we know."

"That's wonderful," I said.

"John was so receptive and full of the Spirit that evening," she added.

"He was a special man," I said.

"He was that way from the moment of his birth. You know, the day he was born I felt some very special feelings, and I was elated for days afterwards. All I wanted to do was just hold him. There was something unique about him. Even as a newborn, he radiated love to everyone around him. Of course that's a mother speaking," she smiled. "But others felt it too. He was a wonderful baby!"

"You know, speaking of babies," I said. "I wish John were going to be here for the birth of this one." I put my hand on my swollen belly.

"He will be," Janet said.

"Do you think so?" I didn't tell her that the thought had already crossed my mind.

"I know my son, and I know how much he loves you. I don't think he would leave you alone at a time like that. Whether he lets you know it or not, I'm certain he'll be there."

But if John was there, I wanted to *know it.* Later that night, when I was alone at home, I prayed for that blessing.

"Father," I said, "I need the comfort of knowing John is at my side when this baby is born. If it be thy will, please, when the time comes, let him be with me, and make me aware of him."

I knew it was a big thing to ask. Communication with loved ones in the spirit world is a rare and sacred thing. Even when John had been near me in the past, somehow I knew it was only by the Lord's grace that it was accomplished. I didn't believe spirits could just come and go at will without entitlement to do so. Surely, there were laws in place that governed that sort of thing. I also came to believe that such communication happens only through the workings of the Holy Spirit.

Because I believed these things, I was even more grateful to the Lord for the times John had spoken to me or had comforted me by his presence. God's mercy had been truly great.

However, I had also come to know the power of faith. My months of study and prayer had caused my faith to increase, and I knew it was possible to bring great things to bear by faith. So when I asked God for Johnny's presence at the birth of our child, I did it in faith, believing that it would be so. And as the weeks continued I tried to repent of all my weaknesses. I served with more diligence in my calling, I turned outward to serve others, returning some of the kindness that had been shown me when John died, and I doubled my sessions at the temple.

Doing these things not only increased my faith that what I had asked for would be granted, but I also experienced immediate benefits as well. The Spirit of the Lord was more often in our home, and the children and I enjoyed many beautiful times together. They felt the Spirit too and were more willing to help me. We had our hard times—the children's still-tender feelings sometimes aggravated differences between them—but our problems resolved themselves quickly, and for the most part, peace reigned in our home.

And over time, something was happening to me that I hadn't expected. My own spiritual strength was developing independently of John. I was coming to have a personal and real relationship with the Lord. It would take a lifetime of effort, and I would have many obstacles yet to overcome, but my hope was growing that someday I *would* be worthy of my own eternal reward—to be at my husband's side in the kingdom of God, and thus bring glory

to our Father in Heaven. In my heart of hearts, there was
nothing I desired more.

One day in the Manti temple, Sister Stephenson
showed Janet and me where she had seen John in the
celestial room. It gave me a sweet feeling to know where
he had been. I would always think of him when in that
special room. And every time, I would sense something
distant, something beyond the moment, something of
John and me together in the realm this room represented.
I felt I would make it there someday if I continued doing
my part. Faith and endurance would keep the way open to
me and one day the love John and I shared would receive
its ultimate fulfillment in that kingdom of glories. Worlds
without end, we would never be parted again.

Chapter Ten

One day towards the end of November, Stephanie came bursting into the house after school.

"Mom!" she yelled.

"In the bedroom!" I called. I was flat on my back in bed with pillows under my knees. My tummy was huge by now and the baby was still transverse. Carrying the baby this way diminished the circulation in my legs. They were swollen and sore. The only way I could get any relief was to lie down. In church the Sunday before, the ladies had looked at me and said, "Chris! Haven't you had this baby yet?" I was embarrassed to tell them I still had three weeks to go. The way I waddled around it was no wonder people thought I was overdue.

Stephanie burst in. "Mom! I won! I won! I beat the whole kindergarten!"

"What did you win?" I asked, sitting up with difficulty.

"The art contest. I get to go to Salt Lake and see the gov'nor and eat dinner."

"That's wonderful," I said, pulling her in for a hug. "I'm so proud of you."

Later I received a phone call from a man who confirmed her story. He said that Stephanie's art work had been selected as the winner from all the kindergartens in the state. We were invited to Salt Lake City on December first for a special banquet with Governor Bangerter.

"I've been told you're expecting a baby," he said. "I hope you'll be able to come."

I had to go. How could I let Stephanie down? Even if I had to go in a rented wheelchair I wouldn't miss it. "We'll be there," I said.

It had been a busy season already. Dr. Jackson thought the baby might come early, and I had done all of my Christmas shopping just in case. But there was still much left undone, not only to prepare for the holiday but for the baby as well. The banquet was a week away. I set that date as my goal to finish getting everything ready.

That week was a whirlwind. I called Lorna and she helped me set up the crib in my room and launder all of the baby things—blankets, sheets, towels, clothes—everything I had in pink. We went shopping and bought plenty of diapers, baby wipes, lotion, and other supplies as well as some cute baby outfits that were warm. This was a December baby, I didn't want her getting cold. We unpacked the Christmas decorations, reorganized some of the closets, and checked the list of gifts for the children one last time. In spite of my advancing pregnancy, it was the most productive week I'd had in a long time. The awkward way I had to carry myself made any movement difficult, and my abdomen and sides were continually wracked with pain from overstretched muscles and ligaments. Also, the swelling in my legs was getting worse. But with Lorna's help I accomplished almost everything on my list.

Later in the week, I had another appointment with Dr. Jackson. He listened to the heartbeat and checked the baby's position.

"Good news, Chris. The baby is starting to drop and its position has improved. The head is coming down."

"That's great!" I said. "Does this mean I won't have to have it Cesarean?"

"Probably—we'll have to see. It looks very promising though."

This *was* good news. I had been praying for the baby to turn. I knew how long it would take to recover from a C-section, and I didn't want to be incapacitated for Christmas. This would be our first Christmas without John and I wanted it to be as perfect as possible for the kids.

"Do you still think the baby will come early?" I asked.

"Maybe so," he said. "A week early, judging by how soon it has dropped."

I was thrilled. My babies never came early. And to avoid a C-section—this was the break I needed.

"What about these pains?" I asked, knowing there was little hope to be rid of them.

"Just stay off your feet," he said.

Thanks Doc, I wanted to say as I got up to leave. *You try taking care of five kids, getting a house ready for a baby and for Christmas, all while lying down.* But the news about an early delivery had made me happy and I left knowing this was going to be my easiest delivery.

The night of the banquet came. John's brother Robert stood in for Stephanie's dad, and Grandma Monsen went too. It was a terrific event. The banquet room of the Marriott Hotel was decked out in fancy linen and crystal, and the meal was lavish. Stephanie glowed all evening in her new, fancy dress. She shook hands with the governor and was presented two trophies, a big one for her school and a smaller one for herself. I saw her artwork for the first time—it was even better than she had described. I was so proud of her. She was so excited that afterwards it took her a long time to settle down and go to sleep.

With the banquet behind me, there was nothing standing in the way of having my baby. Dr. Jackson said the baby was in perfect position now and wouldn't be long in coming. So I packed a suitcase for the hospital and alerted the extended family that the time was near. I asked Lorna if she would drive me in case no one else was available. I was expecting signs of labor to begin any time.

That night at bedtime, I shared the news with the children. We were all gathered in the living room for family prayer.

"Dr. Jackson says the baby will be here soon," I said. "Isn't that great?"

"And we think it is going to be a girl. Right?" Stephanie asked.

"I think it's a girl," I said. "It's what I'm planning for." John had wanted another boy to even the score, but we would see. "Would you like another sister?" I asked.

"Yes," she said, "but I would like it if we had a boy too. This is our *special* baby."

Over the months we had had many talks about our special baby. I had made sure the children remembered that it was mine *and daddy's* baby, that mommy couldn't have one all by herself. Everyone looked forward to its birth with excitement. We knew that the baby would be a constant reminder to us of our dad. I shared with them what I knew about the child: that it had a special spirit and had visited with John in the premortal world.

"Can I feel it?" asked Jennifer.

Everyone rushed to place their little hands on my tummy. They had been so excited in the past to feel it move. But tonight the baby was still.

"Maybe she's asleep," said Michael.

"Or maybe Daddy is talking to her," said Melanie. "Does he talk to her all the time?"

"I don't think so. Maybe only when it's important," I said. I had felt the possibility that the baby's spirit could move in and out of the developing fetus, but I wasn't sure. I *was* sure that John had somehow spent time with it on more than the one occasion he had told me about. I felt a connection between their spirits. Johnny was its father, after all.

"Daddy loves our baby," said Jennifer.

"Yes, he does," I said. "Daddy loves all his children."

Later, in the prayer, Stephanie prayed that the baby would come so that I would not be sick anymore. I said a loud "Amen" to that one.

Days went by and nothing happened. The pulling pains were worse now and it was difficult to sleep. Every day I prayed that the baby would come soon and that everything would go well. "And Father," I always added, "I need John there. I ask in faith, knowing it's possible. Please let him come to me for the delivery."

More days lapsed and I went crazy finding ways to pass the time. I started going through every room of my house, cleaning out the cupboards and drawers, closets, and shelves. My house was never so organized.

"Why won't this baby come?" I prayed one night. "Please, *let this baby come.*" And still I felt nothing that even resembled labor. I was beginning to feel desperate. I couldn't wait much longer.

But another day came and went. Then another, and my pain worsened.

"Well, Chris," Dr. Jackson said during one of my appointments. "This is how it is sometimes. You think things are progressing nicely then it all slows down again. The baby is okay. That's the main thing."

"But *I'm* not! I'm in pain! And I want to get this over with so it won't interfere with Christmas."

"I know, but the best thing to do is let nature take its course, unless there are complications, and I don't see any now that the baby has turned."

I went home feeling despondent. I called Lorna.

"I can't stand this waiting," I told her. "I can't even get a decent night's sleep anymore."

"I know it's tough," she said. "Do you want me to come over and stay with you?"

"No. Just pray for me that this baby will hurry up and get here so I can recover in time for Christmas."

She said she would pray for me and we hung up.

"This is too much!" I cried that night in my own prayers. "Lord, please take me out of this misery. The baby is ready to come and I'm ready to have it. Won't you please let it happen soon? Tonight? I would be so grateful if it came tonight." But I lay there in agony hour after hour, feeling not even the smallest twinge of labor. It was a difficult, endless night.

The next morning I awoke with a start. Sunlight streamed through the window above the empty crib. I sat up and felt a warm sensation growing in my bosom. Then the walls and ceiling seemed to fade as a light, brighter than the sun, filled my room. The warmth continued to spread through me until I was cloaked in a blanket of comfort and peace. John was there—though I didn't see him. With him, I sensed, was another strong presence, another male spirit, but I didn't know who he was.

"Chris," John said in that familiar voice that I loved so much. "Don't rush things. The baby needs time. Its spirit needs to receive final instructions from the Lord."

The words rippled through me like crystal waters. "Have patience. Your prayers will be answered. Just have faith. When the time is right, you will know. Remember, our child needs to receive its instructions first."

I felt John's love surround me.

"Chris," he continued, "I love you. Just remember to have faith."

I started to ask who was with him, but the light started to fade and John and his companion were gone. In a moment the room was back to normal, but I was left with a sublime feeling of happiness and the assurance of John's love.

My pains seemed to diminish for a while as I sat there pondering what had occurred. Have faith and patience, John had said. Faith in the purposes of the Lord, that he was in charge here. Faith that there was a greater plan in motion than I could see. All I had known was discomfort and anxiety, wanting this baby to come according to my own schedule. But I understood now that I was not the only participant in this process. Things were in motion on both sides of the veil and the two were intimately connected. I had prayed for John to be involved with this delivery, and now I saw that he was—on the other side. The baby's spirit was involved too, in a way I had not considered.

"My Heavenly Father," I prayed, "I thank thee for sending my husband, and for what has been made known to me. Forgive me for asking for things that were not according to thy will. Help me have greater patience and faith in thee."

On December twelfth I went in to see Dr. Jackson.

"The pains are getting unbearable," I told him. "I wish there was a way to ease them."

"There is," he said, "have this baby!"

"That's easy for *you* to say."

"It is, isn't it?" he said. "It's too bad babies come only when *they* are ready, and not when you want them to."

These words rang in my mind and echoed John's. *Don't rush things. The baby needs time.*

"We could schedule a C-section for you," he said.

"No," I said. "I've waited this long, I can wait a little longer. I would never recover from a C-section in time for Christmas."

"Well, I think it will be over soon," he said. "If the baby doesn't come in a week, you better come back in. That would be the nineteenth."

The nineteenth! I thought. If I don't have this baby by then, I'll wait until *after* Christmas!

I was upset as I left the doctor's office. It was difficult to have no control over my situation. I was frustrated and weary. But John's words came into my mind again. *Have faith. When the time is right, you will know.* I had to remember there was a divine purpose at work. I had to quit being so selfish.

On the way home I decided that if I wasn't going to have my baby that day, I might as well do something else. When I got home, I loaded some Christmas presents into the car and drove to my mother's house. She was tending Jennifer, Michael, and Clint. We sat at the dining room table and wrapped gifts until it was time for Melanie and Stephanie to come home from school.

"I love wrapping presents," Mom said. "It really gets me in the mood."

"Same here," I said. "Christmas has always been my favorite time of year. Johnny's too."

"You're going to miss him this Christmas."

I nodded. "It will be hard. Our first one without

him. But you know something?"

"What?"

"In a way, I'm anxious for Christmas this year," I said. "Not just for the presents and the lights and the excitement, but because I feel closer to the Lord than I have before. He's been there a lot for me since John died." I finished wrapping the last present and set it with the others ready to take home. "I just hope this baby comes in time to let me really get into the Christmas spirit."

"What does the doctor say?" she asked.

"He says any day now, but he's been saying that for weeks."

We gathered the presents and carried them to my car.

"Isn't there anything Dr. Jackson can do to speed things up?" she asked.

"Not really. Things have to happen in their own time. But I'm ready to throw in the towel. I don't think I can last another day!"

But I did. After that day with my mother, I lasted another *four* days, and on each one I hoped *that* would be my baby's birthday. But none of them were, and my endurance was worn threadbare.

On the fifth day, I woke up and couldn't believe I was still in my bed and not in the hospital. It was the seventeenth, the original due date. The baby's final instructions were certainly taking their own sweet time. I can't stand this anymore, I thought. I'm going to get some contractions started today, or else! And after getting the girls off to school, I started scrubbing my house like a mad woman. I scoured the floors, wiped the walls, washed the windows and the cupboards. No nook or cranny was safe from my cleansing fury. The house sparkled by evening. It was immaculate.

And still I felt no hint of labor.

All night long I tossed and turned. My swollen legs ached. The muscles in my back were aflame. And the pulling pains drove me wild. They were as excruciating as the ones I had with Clint which led to a Cesarean. But Dr. Jackson had said this baby was now in a good position. Had it turned back again? It couldn't have. I would not go through another Cesarean birth, not so close to Christmas and not without John.

The pain and the anxiety were more than I could bear. In the early light of morning I fell to my knees in tears.

"Heavenly Father," I cried, "it's a week before Christmas. I can't have a Cesarean section. Please let me have a normal delivery and let my baby come so I can recover in time. I know that thou livest, and lovest me, and hast always heard my prayers. Please finish the baby's preparations so it can come. I need thy help and I need John's help. Let me deliver today."

The anguished words continued to pour out of me as the morning light grew. I was in turmoil, not wanting to pray for something that was wrong to ask, and yet I felt I simply could not endure another day, another hour. In faith, I prayed from my heart, knowing that the Lord would understand and forgive me if I were praying amiss.

In answer to my prayer the warm glow of the Spirit poured over me. I knew my prayer had been heard and that the Lord *did* understand my feelings. He had been there all along, as John had helped me see, and he would now make things work for my good if I would trust in him. This impression was enough to bring me comfort and strength to keep trying.

As I stood up, the sharpest pain yet raced across my back and around to my stomach. It was a contraction! I ran to the phone and called Dr. Jackson's nurse and asked her to talk to the doctor for me. "I think my contractions have begun. Could you ask him if I should come in?"

She was gone for a minute, but came back and said, "Chris, Dr. Jackson said he should probably check on you. Can you come down?"

"Yes, I'll be there shortly," I said and hung up. A feeling welled up inside of me. This was it. I knew it was. Johnny had said I would know it when the time was right. This was not going to be just a check up. My baby was coming today!

I phoned John's mom with the news and asked her to tend the children, then went in to wake up the kids.

Melanie and Stephanie were out of school for Christmas vacation. I went to their room and got them up.

"Come on, you guys. Everybody up! We've got to get you ready to go to Grandma Monsen's house." I opened their drawers and started to pull clothes out.

Melanie sat up rubbing her eyes. "Why are we going to Grandma's?" she asked.

"The baby is coming today!" I said.

"Today?" She was wide awake now.

"Yes. The doctor says he wants me to come in. Get dressed and help me pack."

We got everyone ready, packed, and then ate breakfast. I called my mom to let her know and then did the dishes and went one last time around the house putting it in order. I wanted a perfect house to bring the baby home to. A few more contractions came—they were mostly in my back—but they didn't slow me down. In fact, they spurred me on. I started moving even faster. We loaded the car and I grabbed my own suitcase which I felt had been sitting by the door for weeks. Then we headed around the corner to Grandma's house.

"Chris, are you going to be okay?" Janet asked. "Are you sure you don't want someone to go with you?"

"No. I'll be fine," I said. "I'll call you later when I know something definite." And I left for the doctor's office, which was adjacent to the hospital in Fillmore. I was glad that I was able to drive myself. I wanted to go to the hospital alone. I knew John would be there for me and I wanted the experience to be a private one.

By the time I got to the office I was having contractions every fifteen minutes. They took my blood pressure. It was high. Then we went across to the hospital for a sonogram. I was relieved when the doctor saw that the baby was in good position with its head pushing straight down towards the birth canal.

"Do you want to stay and we'll have a birthday today?" he asked.

"Yes, I brought my suitcase," I said. "I planned on staying."

"I thought so," he said with a smile. "Everything's going to be fine, Chris," he said and put his hand on my arm. "Try to relax and we'll take care of everything for you. You let me know if there's anything you want."

"Thank you," I said, but what I wanted was to know that John was there. So far, I didn't sense that he was.

Dr. Jackson helped me get my suitcase from the car. On the way to the hospital labor room, I had another contraction—a strong one that gained intensity as it came. It brought back all my fears of having to go through labor alone.

John! I cried out in my mind. I need you!

Once in the room, a nurse helped me into a gown and onto the bed, then strapped an electronic sensor around my belly. I watched the baby's heartbeat light up the graph on the screen and was reassured to see this sign of the tiny life inside me. I loved this baby with all my heart and couldn't wait to hold it in my arms.

The room was pleasantly decorated like a child's room, with little stuffed animals sitting on a wooden chest and a huge easy chair in one corner that was meant for the husbands to sit in while their wives were in labor. I felt lonely seeing the empty chair. John had sat in that very spot when Clint was born.

The nurse brought me some ice to chew on and I tried to relax. The contractions were coming more regularly now but were short-lived. I tried to find a comfortable position on the bed but with no success. A nurse came in with an extra pillow and eased it behind me.

"Would you like something to read or should I turn on the TV?" she asked.

"No, thank you," I said. I thought about asking her to turn on some music, but decided against it. I was expecting John to come and didn't want anything to interfere.

The contractions continued and were getting quite strong until suddenly it seemed they were slowing down. More and more time lapsed between each one until they simply stopped. A nurse came in and checked the monitor. The baby's heartbeat was still strong and regular. We waited for another contraction but they had ceased. She called Dr. Jackson.

"Everything seems okay, Chris," the doctor said after he checked me. "The baby is doing fine."

"So why no contractions?" I asked. "What's happening?"

"I don't know. Let's give it a little more time and we'll see," he said and left.

John, where are you? I thought. Something's not right.

More time passed without contractions and the doctor came back and decided to start me on some Pitocin, a hormonal fluid that causes the muscles in the uterine walls to contract.

"Let's try and jump-start you," he said and smiled.

A nurse came in and hung the bottle of clear liquid on a rack above my head. Then she inserted a needle into a vein on my arm and attached the tube from the bottle. She made an adjustment and the Pitocin started dripping into the tube; I felt something cold inside the vein where the needle entered. It took a little while, but soon the contractions returned. And when they did, they came on strong and hard.

Real labor is a frightening thing. When it grabs you in its iron grip there is no time off, no getting out of it, and no going back until it squeezes the baby free. It's a force of nature completely out of your control, and it can scare you with its power. The contractions were getting more severe and more frequent, and I began to feel afraid.

I tried to sense if John were near, but felt nothing. *Does he know I'm here?* I felt so alone.

When our first baby, Melanie, was born, John had never left my side. There were complications, but he coached me through them, helped me with my breathing, timed each contraction. And when she was born, he said, "Oh no, Chris. What are we going to do? She looks just like me." And she did—red hair and all. But he fell in love with her and would peek in on her first each time he visited us in the hospital. Then once we were home, I couldn't get out of bed, and so Johnny did the diapering. When I finally was able, he would watch me fumble and then say, "Here. Let me do it." Always the perfectionist, Johnny had become the Diapering Pro.

When I was in labor with Stephanie, our second child, John was just as helpful. He held my hand through the whole thing, keeping a broad smile pasted on his face, and saying, "You're tough, Chris. You can do it."

I would give anything to see that smile now and hear those words again.

I thought of Jennifer, our third to be born natural— without medication. John was the Lamaze Pro by then, and he told me to concentrate on his words and do exactly what he said. The delivery was painful but went smoothly because of his coaching. "It's mind over matter," he drilled into me. It worked. We were a team.

Things had gone well with Michael too, until Johnny fainted. Dr. Jackson was our doctor by then and used epidurals. He gave me one when I had Clint too, which helped with the pain, but then I had complications and we opted for surgery. John never left my side then either, toughing out the C-section in the delivery room with me.

So where was he now? I wanted to know. I prayed and asked the Lord to send Johnny to me, but the heavens seemed shut.

Sometime later my parents arrived. They asked how things were going.

"Pretty slowly," I said. "I'm glad you came, I need someone to talk to."

"The nurse says your contractions are regular now," said Mom. "Do they hurt?"

Before I could say "You've done this before, what do *you* think?" another one started up and she could see for herself how much they hurt. The pain increased in intensity. The muscles in my abdomen and along the walls of my uterus worked in tandem, constricting, pushing down harder and harder on the baby until they reached a peak. I tried to breathe through it, to relax and let my muscles do their job. But the pain was too great. I couldn't help catching my breath and gritting my teeth. Then the contraction was over.

My parents stayed for a while, and we spoke between contractions. But I was in a lot of pain, and I knew I was becoming lousy company.

A nurse came in and took my blood pressure. It was higher.

"Are your contractions painful?" she asked.

I said they were.

"Good. That means progress!" she smiled and left.

A while later Dr. Jackson returned. "I hear you're hurting," he said.

"Yes. A lot," I said.

My parents stepped out while he checked me. I was dilated to three.

"Well, you're slow but things are moving," he said. "I'm sorry it hurts, Chris. But I don't think we should give you anything yet. I'll check in again later."

The hours dragged on. The Pitocin continued to drip, and the pains got worse. My dad sat next to me and tried to talk about anything that would keep my mind off the labor. I responded as best I could, but my mind was on John. He still had not come.

This is the time, John, I thought. This is when I wanted you with me—during the hard part. Why don't you come?

The doctor returned and my parents stepped out again. I had made very little progress so the doctor used an instrument to carefully break my water. As it gushed out I felt the baby flip and move downward. After that, the contractions became more localized at the top and front of my tummy where they caused the muscles to bunch and knot. My whole belly felt locked in a giant charley horse.

My parents returned and tried again to comfort me. But it had been eight hours now and I was losing patience. The baby's heartbeat started to speed up. I was becoming more tense and afraid. And I could see that my parents were getting nervous.

A nurse came in to check me.

"I feel something," she said. "It feels like . . . a foot or something."

A foot! No!

"I'll call Dr. Jackson." She left.

The doctor rushed in, checked me, and said, "Chris, I need to see what is happening here. I can feel either an elbow or a foot. I know the baby's turned the wrong way, but I need to see which way. I'm ordering an X-ray."

The baby had flipped when my water broke and was now stuck in some impossible position. I felt a scream rising in my throat. With Clint an elbow and shoulder got stuck in the birth canal. Dr. Jackson had taken him by emergency C-section. This can't be happening again! What about the easy delivery I was expecting? John! Is this your fault? Are you talking again to this child, and delaying this birth? It better be for a good reason.

Dr. Jackson checked the monitor. It was obvious that the baby was undergoing some stress.

"Chris," my dad said, "uh . . . your mother and I are going to leave you for a little while. I think you need some privacy here and we need to get something to eat."

My emotions were out of control and I got angry. How could you leave me? I thought. How dare you! But I was really angry at John. I had tried so hard to merit the blessing of having him with me. I had prayed and exercised my faith. Wasn't it enough? He had better be feeding the five thousand somewhere, I thought, to leave me here like this.

They wheeled the X-ray machine in and I had to hold myself awkwardly for the pictures. The contractions were so painful in that position, I thought I was having the baby right then. Then we had to wait for the X-rays to come back.

The first X-rays weren't clear enough, and the doctor returned to take two more. The contractions were getting closer together. If they don't hurry up, I thought, I'm going to have this baby breech!

My parents returned and I wanted to cry. I needed their comfort. John's parents also came by the room to let me know they were there. My dad had phoned and told them I was having difficulties.

The strain of labor was draining me. Between contractions I slumped back into the pillows like a dead fish, my eyes rolling back in my head. But my mind never rested. Why was this happening? Oh, John! How I need you! Our baby's in trouble, John. *Do something!* Heavenly Father, help me!

Finally the doctor returned. "Chris, the baby is turned sideways. We'll have to take it Cesarean."

No! It wasn't supposed to be this way! But I would do anything at this point for the safety of the baby.

I nodded my head.

My parents left and an anesthesiologist came in to give me an epidural. He pulled the bed away from the wall and got behind me. He held the huge needle that he would use to inject fluid into my spinal cord and make me numb from the waist down. It should have been an easy procedure—it had worked well with Michael and Clint—but the anesthesiologist had trouble getting the needle into my back. He stuck me again and again without success. Then he started up my spine trying to insert the needle between every vertebrae.

Stop, I wanted to scream. My back felt like a pin cushion.

The monitor showed the baby was undergoing a lot of stress by now. Soon its life would be in danger.

He kept trying to insert the needle, working from every angle and position, but he hit bone with every jab. And my contractions were coming one right after the other, overwhelming me with pain. Every muscle in my body constricted sharply with each jab. It was agony.

Dr. Jackson broke in, "No more," he said. "We can't wait any longer. We'll just have to give her some general anesthesia and knock her out."

The anesthesiologist agreed, and I had to admit, that sounded good to me too.

It was sometime before 9:00 PM when they tugged me onto a gurney and thrust the gurney out the door towards the operating room. The nurses and technicians moved quickly, knowing this was critical. Everything was moving so fast. I felt that I wanted a priesthood blessing, but I didn't dare ask. The baby's life was at stake now. There was no time for a blessing.

When they lifted me onto the operating table I tried to look around to sense if John could be there. The room was totally void of his presence and oh, so cold. Another contraction twisted my body and every impulse in my being screamed to bear down hard and push that baby out. I felt the baby kick me as if it were fighting for its life and I started crying uncontrollably. They had to help my baby! Please, help my baby!

I was covered with sweat and trembling with cold. And I never felt more alone and betrayed in my life.

John, you didn't come. *Why didn't you come?*

Everyone rushed to their places and the anesthesiologist wheeled his equipment in next to my head. While he was getting a syringe ready, the nurses strapped my arms and wrists down with tape. The operating lights burst on and the rest of the room plunged into darkness.

This is it, I thought, and I waited for the gas mask to cover my face and bring blackness and relief to my battered body and soul.

Chapter Eleven

$\mathcal{M}$rs. Monsen," the anesthesiologist said into my ear. "I'm going to give you a shot to make you sleepy. You'll feel just a little sting...there."

I felt the needle go into my arm and pull out.

"Now I'm putting a mask over your mouth and nose."

I felt the plastic mask rest on my face.

"Close your eyes and breathe deeply."

I did as he said.

"Now, I want you to count backwards from ten with me."

"Ten, nine," I counted.

"Slowly."

"Eight...seven...six..."

"That's right...You should feel it working now."

I felt drowsy. Noises in the room sounded far away.

"Five...four..." I was slowing down. I couldn't pronounce the words.

"Three..." I was drifting...
"Two..." It was a whisper...

"Chris..."
A familiar voice...
"Chris..."
I slowly opened my eyes.
"I'm here, Chris."
I turned to see.
It was John.
"Johnny!"

He stood a short distance from me. An immense brightness radiated from him.

"Oh! John!" I ran towards him, not noticing that I wasn't lying down, that the mask was missing from my face, that I was no longer in the operating room. It was my husband! Nothing else mattered. I just had to get to him.

"John!" I cried and threw myself into his arms. He wrapped them tightly around me. "John. John." I buried my face in his neck and wept.

"Chris." He held me, saying my name over and over. "Chris, it's okay. You're with me." His words and his touch melted my anguish. The pain and terror of childbirth faded away.

"John, I can't believe I'm holding you," I said. "Is this real?"

"Yes, Chris. It's real."

I held him more tightly and felt his hands caress my back and shoulders in that, oh, so familiar way. His spirit body was solid to my own spirit's touch. This *was* him.

This was really *him!* The hurt and loneliness that had haunted me released its grip and ebbed away. I was back in the arms of the one I loved. Peace settled into my heart. Still cradled in his embrace, I asked, "Where were you? Why didn't you come when I needed you?"

"I'm sorry, Chris, I couldn't. The Lord wanted to bless you by bringing you here, but we had to wait for the right moment. I've been here all along, waiting for you."

I looked up into his face and found it free of wrinkles. He was young and vibrant. His eyes, looking deep into mine, sparkled with life.

He smiled. "Do you know where you are?"

I pulled away and looked. Oh! The glory of the scene that met my eyes! An elegant, spacious garden enveloped us. It abounded with flowers, shrubs, and trees of every kind. Brooks sparkled among the greenery, and crystal pools shimmered beneath the spreading boughs of trees. Beyond the garden endless fields stretched into infinity. Arrayed across them like living drifts of snow were masses of white flowers. They were daylilies, the color of ivory and pearl and white marble. Their heads swayed with gentle breezes that transported their delicate perfume throughout the landscape. Beyond the fields of lilies, mountains lifted their majestic peaks high into a vast sky.

"John," I gasped. "It's beautiful. Look at the colors!" The scene was ablaze with living color as if a tiny sun burned within each particle of every leaf, flower, and fountain of grass. Even the mountains radiated a resplendent glow.

I turned to him. "This is heaven," I said.

"It's what you know as the spirit world. This is just a tiny corner of it," he said.

I realized that we were conversing through thoughts without using our mouths.

"Am I dead?" I asked.

"No, Chris, you're just passing through. I'm so *proud* of you. Do you realize it was your own faith that made this possible?"

"But, John, I want to stay. I can't leave you!" I brought my hands up to his chest. "You look wonderful, Johnny. You look so... happy." It was the only word I could come up with. I had never seen him this content. I sensed his strength and confidence. He was utterly at peace with himself.

"Chris, we don't have much time," he said.

The fabric of John's robe under my hands was luminescent. "Look at your robe," I said. "It's so white it shines!" It glistened, reflecting light like satin or taffeta, but also possessed an inner light of its own.

"Chris..."

"I've never seen anything like this." I slipped my hand under a fold to feel it better between my fingers.

"Chris!" John said firmly. "Please listen to me. We don't have a lot of time together and there are lots of things to talk about. Try to quit thinking in earthly terms and understand what I have to say."

I sensed his firmness but also his great love for me.

He looked softly into my eyes and smiled. "I have so much to tell you," he said.

Oh, my Johnny. I was in absolute awe of this magnificent man who stood gazing into my eyes. Take the John I knew in life with all of his energy, wit, and open-heartedness and magnify him a hundredfold; purify his masculinity and grace; add worlds of knowledge, intelligence, and wisdom; throw in complete self-confidence and self-mastery and you would have this noble, brilliant spirit in front of me now. Yet he was still my Johnny. The essence of his personality had not changed—in fact it had developed. He was more himself than I knew him to be in life.

A sad memory of him came to mind. "John," I said. "It was a terrible thing to watch you die. I couldn't save you."

He drew me closer to him. "Chris..."

"I'm sorry." I said and buried my face in his shoulder. "Why did it happen, Johnny?"

"There are things for me to do here, Chris, that no one else can do. Every being has a unique purpose and... I have to fulfill mine."

"Why now?" I asked, searching his eyes.

"Because I accomplished everything I was on earth to do. Timing is important in the Lord's plan, and... it was my time. The Lord carries out his plans perfectly, Chris. *He* called me home."

I leaned forward touching my forehead to his chest. "He needed you more than I did," I said—not in bitterness, but in understanding and acceptance.

"No, Chris." He put his hands on my shoulders and extended his arms so he could look me in the eye. "Have faith! God knows what's best for *you, too.* Your living without me on earth is just as purposeful as my being here. He loves you no less than he loves me." He smiled. "Trust him. He knows perfectly what you need, because he knows you perfectly."

He took my hands in his. "When I died, I came through the darkness to a light. Jesus Christ was waiting there for me. He reached out his arms and I went to him. He called me by name and I knew that there was nothing about me he didn't know. He had known me since before the age in which the earth was formed, had known me and been aware of me and loved me all along. And when we were reunited it was with *tremendous joy.* He knows *you*, Chris, in the same way."

John was sharing with me not only his thoughts but his feelings. As he described his joy, I felt it surge through my being like a quick charge of light, infusing me with happiness. And when next he spoke of Christ's love for him, I felt that, too.

"He enfolded me in his love," John said. "Oh, Chris, Jesus' love is miraculous! On earth the only emotions you feel are your own, even in sympathy with others. But here, that's not so. I felt a portion of Christ's own emotions, and so there was no questioning. I knew by my own experience how deeply and perfectly he loves me. This shattered my fears and wiped away my pain. I felt comforted like never before."

My own heart overflowed with serenity and love, and I said, "John, I want to feel this way forever." I hugged him. "I never want to leave this place—or you."

"You can feel this comfort, Chris, in your own world—at least a portion of it. Jesus' mercy is great. He *is* your brother and he wants you to draw near to him. If you do, he will draw near to you, and you will feel his comfort and his love."

"I have felt it, John," I said. "Often he comforts me when I grieve for you. We have felt his Spirit in our home."

John nodded. "He promised to watch over you."

"When you agreed to stay?"

"Yes. I was given the choice, but I didn't bargain with the Lord. His promise to watch over my family was the blessing that came from choosing the better way. I chose it because I was shown the results of both choices."

He drew me to his side and we walked down a grassy path. Faint music sounded around us—it seemed nearby but also far away.

"Who is singing?" I asked.

"The angels. I love to hear them praising God!"

I listened. The music was beautiful and serene. "How long can I stay, John?"

"Not long," he said.

I stopped walking. "Then there are some things I need to know."

"What, Chris?"

"John, what's going to happen to us? Is my place with you assured? If I leave you, will I find my way back?"

He looked out at the fields of white lilies and said, "Ah, sweet wife, I want you to know something." He looked back at me. Excitement filled his face. "Temple marriage is *real. Our* temple marriage is real, Chris. We are sealed as husband and wife *forever*. What was bound on earth *is* bound in heaven, and what we felt the day we were married is true; our union was meant to be. We're eternal companions."

"But will I make it, John?" I pleaded. "Will I endure to the end? I love you so much, I have to know. How could I ever leave this place without knowing I'll see you again?"

He stepped nearer and placed his hands on my shoulders. My mind exploded into a thousand flashing images, and I was shown my future. I also saw many things pertaining to our children and their futures. And there were other things I wanted to know as well. What was John's work in the spirit world? What had he experienced there? What was the rest of this world like? He answered these questions and more, as quickly as they formed in my head. I was not overwhelmed or confused by so many images exploding one after another. My mental capacity seemed unlimited, and I understood everything I saw with pure comprehension.

The images ended, and I came away enthralled and amazed.

"You won't remember these things," he said. "Only that you've witnessed them and that they gave you hope. If you were to remember what you've seen, you wouldn't act according to your own agency, and your purposes on earth would be thwarted."

"Then I'll have to live by faith," I said.

"Yes, Chris. *Faith.* So much of life is designed to help us develop faith. It's more important than you can imagine."

John had told me that it was by my faith I was brought to this world. Then faith was surely a potent thing, and a little bit takes a person a long way. But I had worked hard for my faith. "How much faith do I need?" I asked.

"You need more faith than it takes to move a mountain," he said. "You have to develop that kind of faith because of what's ahead of you. It's not just for yourself, it's for our children, too."

"Because of their missions in life."

"Yes, they are capable of accomplishing great things. You must raise them close to the gospel. It's *so* important." He took me by the hand. "Chris, I want you to listen very carefully to what I'm going to say."

Then he led me gently by his side along a path through a stand of trees. The smooth trunks extended lithely upwards through thick layered leaves. A tiny stream produced delicate tones as it dipped and swirled near the path.

As we walked, he continued speaking. "These will be my most important instructions. You must try your hardest to live by them, because they'll see you and the children through the terrible turmoil ahead. They will also secure our family's eternal reward—something you know I want with *all* my heart." He held my hand in both of his. "I can't always be with you. This is a rare privilege, Chris, for me to speak to you like this, to warn you, and to give you guidelines to follow."

We came to the edge of the trees and stopped. John put one arm around my shoulders and with the other gestured outward. He said, "Look!"

I looked and the veil of heaven parted, and I saw the earth rotating amid the broad expanses of space. I was awed by its size and its grandeur, but it was not the radiant aquamarine sphere that I had seen in pictures. Rather, it was enveloped in layers of dark haze that moved across the planet's face and masked its beauty from my eyes.

"What is that haze?" I asked.

"That is Evil, Chris. It darkens the earth."

"It's growing more thick as we watch."

"The vapors of darkness will continue to spread until the whole earth is covered with filthiness."

I was sickened to see the earth defiled this way. "It's horrifying," I said. "John, I can't return there."

"Don't be afraid," he said. "Days are coming that will cause many hearts to fail, but *you* don't need to fear, Chris. The Lord, Jesus Christ, has power to preserve you. But first you must come to *know* him. Those who know the Lord will be given sanctuary from the wickedness that pollutes the earth."

He turned me to him.

"Chris, you must make Christ your foundation. As the entire structure of a house rests completely on a firm foundation, so the structure of your life must rest completely on Christ. He is the *only* foundation that will not crumble in the times ahead. And you must make his church your cornerstone. The Church is true. Live by its precepts and listen to the words of the prophet. Remember these things. Make Christ your foundation and the Church your cornerstone. Also, study God's word. Pray continually—the power of prayer is real. Attend your meetings faithfully, and have family home evenings. Follow the Spirit. It will lead you aright. These are the only ways to overcome the buffetings of Satan and his forces."

He turned me back and said, "Look again."

Our view of the earth had closed and I saw, once again, the wide vista of the spirit world in which we stood. Only this time, I saw farther and more clearly than before. From the resplendent green grass at my feet to the farthest reaches of the highest mountains, the beauties of the spirit creation spread before me in crystalline splendor.

I wanted to fall to my knees. "It's breathtaking," I whispered.

John gathered me to him. "It is. And it's real and it's here and it's part of an endless realm of love and light where Christ reigns in perfect righteousness. The earth is a speck of dust compared to the heavenly creations! And you see *no* vapors of darkness *here*. Chris, when you go, remember this place as you see it now. Remember *me*, sweetheart. Know that I'm here waiting for you. All of this and more can be ours, together, if you have faith and do what I've said to do."

"I'll remember," I said.

"I know you will. I want you also to teach my words to our children. Give them the keys to happiness I've given you. Tell them how much I love them. Oh, Chris, you and the children are the most precious gifts I have. The Lord will let me watch over you and be there when the children are baptized or blessed or at other special times. But this, too, will be according to your faith, knowing you will be

watched over. I hold all of you dearly in my heart and I
want us to be together in the eternities."

I threw my arms around his neck and bathed his face
with my tears. "Oh, Johnny!" I cried. "I want that, too. But
I can't bear to leave you. I can't do it. I love you too much."

"I know, Chris," he said. "It was hard for *me* to leave
you."

We stood embracing for several minutes, murmur-
ing tender expressions of love. I still couldn't believe I
was here and pressing John close to me. How my empty
arms had ached for him these many months. How my
lonely heart had cried for him. But now, my every loss
was filled by his tender love. As I held him, I felt his love
swell inside of me until it seemed to fill eternities within
me, and I knew our love would never end, that John and
I would be together forever. What joy and peace came
over me then. Conviction that I could go on and raise
his children as he wanted me to secured itself in my
breast.

"Before you go," he said, "I'm going to bless you and
give you strength to do what you must do."

"A priesthood blessing?"

"I know you wanted one before surgery. Would you
like a blessing now?"

"Oh, *yes,*" I said, and we found a place where I could
sit. He took his place behind me, and I bowed my head.
Then I sensed another being drawing near. I did not look
up. I believed it was the same companion who was with
John before, when he came to tell me that the baby
needed time. His companion stood next to John, and they

placed their hands on my head. John called me by name and bestowed a blessing upon me.

In it, he promised me many things. That I would recover quickly from my surgery in time for Christmas. That the swelling in my legs would disappear and be replaced by good circulation. That I would run and not be weary. He blessed me with wisdom and power in my calling as a mother, that I would teach our children well and train them up in the ways of the gospel. He blessed me with understanding concerning the power of the gospel of Jesus Christ to guide me and the children through difficult days to come. He said that I would not remember everything I had seen or learned in the spirit world, but that as I needed it, knowledge would return to me. He promised many things and said that, as I fulfilled my responsibility to our children, these promises would be mine. He said many other things that comforted and strengthened me. When he finished, he closed in the name of Jesus Christ.

His companion drew away. When I raised my head he was gone. Before I could ask who it was, John lifted me to my feet and said, "It's time for you to go, Chris."

"No," I said and held him tight. "I can't let you send me away. I need more time with you."

"But Chris, you have a mission to complete. Our children need you to raise them. I've taught you how."

"Can't I stay a little longer?"

"But the baby, Chris."

"The baby!" I had forgotten to ask about the baby. "Tell me about the baby..."

"This child is a very valiant spirit, saved for these times along with others, and will accomplish a great work for the Lord. It will be a comfort to you, Chris. It will be like me in so many ways—in appearance and mannerism—and will remind you of me always. This last child is my final gift to you and will cause you to think of me and our love—our *eternal* love. This great spirit and I have enjoyed our time together, and we've shared a lot of love. But that's all I can say, Chris. It's time for us to part. You have to return and I have to go back to my duties."

"Not yet, Johnny. Please!"

"I'm sorry, Chris." He took a step away. "Know that I'm happy here and busy with the Lord's work." He smiled. "Don't let me be forgotten. Keep a journal. Record the story of our lives and preserve it along with all of our special experiences here."

He took another step.

"John! No!" I reached for him but he continued on.

"I love you deeply, Chris. And I miss you. We'll be together again."

"*John! I need you!*" I cried.

He stopped and smiled a warm and gentle smile. I felt his love enter my heart and gladden my entire being with the sense that he belonged to me, and in that instant, I knew *he needed me, too.* Then the smile faded and he said, "Chris. *Listen.*"

I listened, and a little way off, I heard a baby cry a strong, healthy cry.

"Sounds like that baby needs its mother," John said.

And I knew that the crying baby was *my* baby. It had been born. I turned back to John. There was nothing on earth that could tear me away from him but this. *I knew I had to leave.* I ran to him and threw my arms around him in one final clutching embrace. "I will always love you, John," I said through my tears, my heart breaking. And we kissed that tender passionate kiss befitting the final farewell of lovers.

"Good-bye, Chris," he said.

Then he was gone.

Chapter Twelve

A nasty, acrid smell invaded my nostrils. The anesthesiologist was holding smelling salts under my nose.

"Stop that!" I yelled and lunged at him. The restraining tape on my arm ripped free, and the unfortunate man received a wallop that sent him sprawling across the floor.

"I don't think she liked that," a nurse said.

"Well, Chris!" It was Dr. Jackson. "That's some backhand! Be careful with him—he's the only anesthesiologist we've got!"

Returning to my body was no joy coming from that world of light and peace, and for an instant, I blamed the anesthesiologist for snatching me back with his vile ammonium carbonate. Take that! I thought, for dragging me from the arms of my husband.

I felt I had never lost consciousness, but my body was full of drugs now—I was groggy, and I couldn't hold my eyelids open. Memories of the spirit world swirled in my head. John! Where did you go?

"Chris," Dr. Jackson said. "Chris, can you hear me?"

His voice tugged me to the surface. "What?" I said without moving my mouth.

"Chris, do you know what you had?"

I nodded. I'd had a baby, I thought. John and I have a new baby.

"Chris, it's a boy. The nurses are cleaning him up now. He's beautiful!"

"A boy..." I mumbled. My mind went hazy. No, I have a girl. Johnny said it was a...I couldn't remember.

"She's still out of it," Dr. Jackson said. "Let's move her to the recovery room."

Once again I floated away on images of that beautiful world, the lofty mountains, the swaying lilies, and John.

When I surfaced again they were wheeling me down the hospital corridor on a gurney.

"Mrs. Monsen," a nurse was saying. "Mrs. Monsen."

I turned my head and half opened my eyes.

"Wake up, Mrs. Monsen. Do you know what you had?" she asked.

"They said...I had...a...baby." Now leave me alone. I wanted to think only of where I had been, only of John.

"Yes, but it was a boy, Mrs. Monsen. Do you know you had a boy?"

"No..."

"Well, you did. He's *perfect*."

I slipped away again, my thoughts passing between this world and the next.

I awoke much later in the recovery room. My mother was next to the bed, and Dad was talking with John's parents near the door.

"Mom," I said.

"Yes, honey. I'm here."

"Something happened." I wanted to tell her everything in a tumble of words describing the spirit world and John. But I was too weak to think how to start. "Something really wonderful..."

"Okay, honey," Mom said, but Lewis had her attention. He was describing something that excited him. He was waving his arms wildly as he spoke.

"The nurse brought him in," Lewis was saying, "and put him in the bassinet. And *that's* when he *did* it."

"Mom," I tried again. "I was in the most beautiful place..."

She wasn't listening.

"*Mom*," I said.

"Yes, Chris. Oh, sweetheart." She took my hand. "Lewis and Janet went down to the nursery and saw the baby."

"You should've seen what he did!" Lewis said from the doorway.

Janet came towards me. "Hello, Chris," she said. "Honey, the baby is *so cute*! He looks so much like John, I can't get over it."

"Looks like John," I repeated.

"Spittin' image of him as a newborn."

"A boy."

"Yes, a beautiful boy. We didn't hold him, though. You get first honors."

Lewis continued. "The nurse laid him in a bassinet."

"It was a warming bed. With lights," Janet corrected him.

"Okay, a *warming bed*. Anyway, she laid him on his *stomach*. And I said to the nurse, 'Will he be okay like that?' And next thing he did a push-up! Like he was saying, 'Yes, I can manage just fine, thank you.' I thought, Look at this kid, just a few minutes old, and he's doin' push-ups!"

A hunger filled my heart. "I want to see him," I said. "Can we ask them to bring my baby?" John had said many wonderful things about the baby, but I was the one who had carried him. I had nurtured him within my body, worried over him, cried over him, prayed for him. I needed him in my arms.

Mothers were usually moved to their own rooms before babies were brought to them, and I was still in recovery. But Janet knew a couple of the nurses. "I'll see what I can do," she said and left.

Dr. Jackson came in.

"How's my boxing champ?" he said.

"I'm fine."

"Well, you shouldn't be. You just had surgery!" He came around and checked my eyes. "But everything went well, Chris. You had a routine C-section. No complications." He put his fingers on my neck and found my pulse. "You had fluid in your stomach, but we cleared it and things proceeded from there."

I didn't say anything to Dr. Jackson about my experience. He didn't seem to know I had been gone during surgery. But I was. My spirit slipped away from my body and I travelled, somehow, through the veil. It wasn't a dream; I was *there* with John—my senses sharpened, my awareness made more keen. How my body had fared so well without me, I didn't know.

He lifted the bedsheet to check my bandages. "That new boy of yours is something else," he said. "Everybody who helped in surgery loves the little guy, the way he came out kickin' and hollerin', so full of life, like 'Here I am world. Stand back!'"

Where's my baby! I wanted to yell. My arms ached to hold him, as they had ached for so many months to hold John. How long had Janet been gone, anyway?

"I checked him over," the doctor continued as he lowered the sheet. "He's all there and in perfect health. Which is more than I can say for you."

I smiled.

"But, considering what you've been through, you do look pretty good. Nothing's wrong with you that a lot of bed rest won't cure."

Just then Janet leaned through the door. She wore a wide grin. "The baby's on his way," she said and pushed open the door.

My heart gave a leap.

"Chris," Dr. Jackson put his hand on my arm. "I'll leave you folks alone, but I want you to know how happy I am for you. I think this little boy is going to fill quite a bit of that empty heart of yours." He looked at both sets of parents and then back to me. "You're in good hands with this cheering section. I'll check back in a little while."

"Thank you, Dr. Jackson," I said.

"You're welcome," He said and left.

I looked expectantly toward the door where Janet still stood holding it open. I tuned all my attention—every sense, every instinct—to this moment. The pain of pregnancy and labor vanished. All I could think of was wanting to hold my baby and to mother him with every whit of energy and love I had. *This child will be a comfort to you, Chris,* Johnny had said, *and is my final gift to you.* I couldn't wait to cradle him and feel that comfort, that bonding, that assurance that he was alive and okay.

"Here he comes!" Janet said, and a moment later a nurse appeared in the doorway. The white bundle in her arms was my baby! An excited hush fell over the room. As she walked in, a warm spirit entered with her, flowing into my heart with a sweet and gentle glow. I knew it meant John was near.

She approached the bed. "There's a handsome young man here to see you," she said.

Behind her, a few other nurses gathered, smiling in the doorway, unable to resist the draw of this special moment. Mom and Dad came near me on the right, and Lewis and Janet moved from the door to the foot of the bed. The nurse carefully shifted the baby from her arms into mine. I brought him close to me. Tears sprang to my eyes. This was a miracle, a wonder, a joy. My baby was finally here.

I gazed at his face and caught my breath. He looked just like John. The same strong chin, the same nose and eyes, and on top of his head, a thick mat of silken red hair that the nurse had combed to one side. With my free hand I touched the side of his tiny wrinkled cheek. "Oh...hello, little one," I said softly. "I heard you crying for me." I tilted my head and kissed his forehead. "I'm here now. Your mommy's here."

My mother whispered, "He *does* look like his dad."

"But he's cuter," my father countered.

Everyone was smiling. The spirit in the room swelled and John's presence surrounded us in love and tranquility. Lewis drew Janet close to him. Tears filled his eyes.

Oh, John, I thought. Your son is beautiful! And you were right—he reminds me of you. I will love you both forever. What a precious gift you have given me.

I imagined John—stately and serene, and striking in his glowing white robe—looking upon this tender scene with immeasurable gladness. I sensed his pride in his son, whom he had known and loved, and maybe had been with not long before my visit to the spirit world. I imagined John bidding farewell to this dear child, wrapping him in his arms, whispering final words of affection and encouragement. Oh, yes. John was happy. His son had finally passed from his arms into mine and had begun his mission.

The baby stretched. He pushed his clenched fists outward and extended his tiny legs. I put my hand on his body where the tiny ribs strained beneath his gown. I saw for myself that he was perfect, that the stress of labor had not left him damaged in any way, and I was relieved.

"You little toad!" I said to him. "You were supposed to be a girl."

He closed his eyes and yawned.

That Johnny! I thought. *He* did this! He let me believe it was a girl when he *knew* all along it *wasn't.* Then it all came together. Every time John had spoken of our child he had called him "it" or "the baby." Very funny! Even in the spirit world, John hadn't let on. Before he died, he had wanted to even the score—three girls, three boys. And then, when he got to the other side and found out the baby *was* a boy, he had launched a scheme to keep *me* planning on a *girl.* You and your last laughs, I thought. Dying hasn't changed you a bit, Johnny Monsen!

After a while, my parents came around the bed to see the baby and touch him while he lay in my arms. Then Lewis and Janet did the same. And then of course, before the nurse returned, the two grandmas had to hold him "*just for a second!*" Finally, the nurses arrived to take the baby. I wanted to keep him, but I was so tired and weak. I knew he would get better care in the nursery than I could give him just then. So I let him go, knowing that because of John's blessing, I would recover quickly and that soon, very soon, the baby would be mine to have and to hold just as long as I wanted.

Shortly, Dr. Jackson authorized my transfer from the recovery room to a private room in another wing of the hospital. When they moved me, Mom, Dad, Janet, and Lewis followed along. What a procession we must have made—the head nurse in front, clutching her clipboard, leading the way. I came next, strapped to a gurney and propelled down the corridor by bustling orderlies. A bevy of nurses followed, wheeling IV bottles on racks and transporting supplies for me and the new room. And trailing behind them—light of step and still jabbering about *what a doll* the baby was—came my four parents. Dr. Jackson had called them my cheering section and so they were. They had seen me through pregnancy and labor with encouragement and cheer rather like four *husbands*. Their place with me was well deserved.

After getting me settled in the new room, Janet and Lewis and my parents stayed just long enough to share their feelings once again about the baby. They sensed in him a special spirit and were so delighted he had come to us. Each one expressed the conviction that John's spirit had attended the baby's birth and that it was an event to treasure the rest of our lives.

I wanted to share my experience with them, knowing how it would touch and comfort them, but I saw that they were tired and ready to leave. This was not the right time. But the day would come soon enough when I *would* share it, when my description of John would comfort Lewis and Janet and give them assurance that their son was happy, vibrant, and busy, when my own parents would be moved by my certain witness that there was a life beyond. For now, it was time for them to go, and each one hugged me and promised to return the next day, "only because we want to see that boy of yours," Lewis joked. Then I watched them leave together, the grandmothers talking excitedly about their new grandson, the grandfathers slapping each other on the back. And I was left alone.

It was late. The nurse made a final check on me and left me propped up by pillows in my bed. I hadn't wanted to go to sleep just yet. The lights in the halls dimmed and the entire hospital grew quiet. Outside my window, the mid-December sky was cold and packed with bright stars. Near my head, a small lamp threw a warm blanket of light across the bed. I picked up a notebook and pen and started to write. I began my record of what had transpired that day. My memories were fresh and vivid and my pen flowed as I recalled easily what I was allowed to remember of all I had seen and heard. I described my reunion with John and the ecstasy I had felt in his presence. As I wrote, I felt again a portion of my emotions while in the spirit world, and tears fell on the bedclothes. My heart had been left tender by so much joy and love. And I felt so much gratitude to the Savior for allowing me this great blessing. I attributed it not to John, but to Him and to His mercy.

Soon, it became clear to me just how special my experience was. It was deeply powerful and was filled with transcending elements that would take a lifetime of pondering to fathom completely. The experience would transform my life, and the lives of others. Suddenly, what the Lord had let me witness in his heavenly realm became a cosmic juncture, a turning point in my eternal existence. I saw that my entire life, up to the moment John pulled me through the veil, was behind me. Now, by the grace of my Redeemer, a new vista had opened up, a new life was spreading itself before me. Like my infant son, by stepping from one world into the next, I had been born anew.

I put some of those thoughts down on the page, then feeling inspired by John's spirit to do so, I used his own words to write a letter from him to his children. In it he expressed his love for them and left his instructions for living their lives in such a way that would assure our togetherness as a family forever. I would give the letter to each child as they were old enough to understand. It would reinforce to them that their daddy lives on and cares about them and wants them to live righteous lives. I wanted them to have a taste, by reading their father's own words, of what I had experienced when I was with him.

When I was too tired to write any more, I laid the pen in the book and set it on the nightstand. I turned off the lamp and let myself relax into the bed. I said a prayer, thanking Heavenly Father for blessing me by bringing my dear son safely into the world. And I thanked him for his own Dear Son, my Lord and Redeemer, Jesus Christ, who through his magnificent grace had allowed me to visit my husband in heaven, who had let me feel the love and supreme peace of that beautiful place. I knew I could not have merited such a grand blessing except for the Savior's atoning love. I committed myself to him and expressed my deep gratitude and love.

After the prayer, my thoughts soon drifted back to John, and I felt myself falling towards a deep and exhausted sleep. But then, something came urgently to my mind. It was a decision I had been faced with since seeing my son for the first time. An answer had suddenly become clear. I turned on the lamp and retrieved the pen and notebook. I opened to a blank page, and at the top, poised my hand to write what I knew, with certainty, was to be the name of my newborn son.

I would name him John. After his father. And his middle name would be Jared, which in Hebrew means *heavenly messenger*. John is also the English version of a Hebrew name. It means *God's gracious gift*.

The next day started with a 7:30 AM visit from Lewis.

"I wanted to come by to take a Polaroid shot of the baby," he said with a sheepish grin. He wanted to show his new grandson off at school that day.

While we waited for the nurse to bring the baby in, Lewis said, "He's a special kid, Chris. Last night I felt John's spirit so strong after the baby was born. And it's a comfort to see how much he looks like John."

"Every time I hold him, I feel comforted," I said.

Lewis continued. "After John died, a huge gap opened in my heart."

I nodded.

"This baby is helping close it," he said.

I smiled, knowing exactly what he was trying to say.

They brought the baby in, and we laid him on the bed. Lewis got a couple of good shots, hugged me, and headed out for work.

When Lorna came to visit, I was so happy to see her.

"I'm having so much fun," I told her.

"Doing what?"

"Calling everyone I know and bragging!" I said. "A new baby is so much fun. Everybody likes to hear about him."

"I'll bet they're all surprised. You told everyone you were having a girl."

"I know," I said. "I'm going to call Mom and tell her to buy him some clothes. All I brought with me are girl things. I can't take him home in pink! John would die. He'd want him to wear, you know, something with footballs on it."

We laughed. And later I told her some of my experience, and we hugged and cried. Lorna knows my heart, and she understood perfectly everything I said.

Later, John's mom called to see how I was doing. "Have you decided what to name him?" she asked.

"Yes, I have, Janet. His name is John Jared Monsen."

"Oh, that's wonderful! I'm so happy." Her voice cracked and I could tell she was crying. "What are you going to call him?"

"Johnny."

She was silent. I knew she was thrilled and touched. Janet always expressed her joy in tears instead of words.

Dr. Jackson came to see me.

"Chris! You're looking good today."

"Thanks. I feel great."

"Glad to hear it. Let's have a look at the swelling in your legs."

He pulled back the covers.

"Chris . . ." he said. "There's *no swelling* here. Look at your ankles, they're normal. What did you do? This is amazing."

I smiled, knowing this was the result of John's blessing. It was a tangible witness to me that what I had experienced was real and true.

Before he left, he gave me instructions to massage my uterus down to size, or else "the nurses will come in here and massage it good and hard *for* you." Doctors always made this threat.

"Oh-kay." I rolled my eyes.

I decided to curl my hair and put on makeup. I was surprised at how easily I walked around the room. After Melanie was born I couldn't walk for a week. I'd had trouble with circulation in my legs then, too.

After I was cleaned up I felt great. Things were going along smoothly, not like the day before. But I harbored no bitterness about what I had suffered. Now I understood why labor had been so difficult. The C-section was a small price to pay for the chance to see John and to touch him. I hoped I would always remember this lesson: When times are the toughest, don't get discouraged. God may be fixing to do something wonderful.

And wonderful is the best word to describe what it was like when, later in the day, Mom and Dad showed up with all of my children.

"Mommy! Mommy!" they cried as they charged into the room. But I was soon forgotten when they noticed little Johnny lying in my arms.

"Ooooh . . . our new baby." They became almost reverent.

"Is he sleeping?"

"Can I hold him?"

They gathered around me in as tight a circle as they could possibly manage. To keep them from poking and prodding, I had to unwrap the baby and let everyone hold his hand and touch his feet and toes.

"Ha! Look at his tiny fingernails!" Stephanie said.

"*Gently,*" I reminded Michael when he got a little rambunctious bending one of Johnny's feet back and forth.

"His diaper is so little, Mommy." Melanie was used to seeing Clint's toddler diapers.

"Can we wake him up?" Jennifer wanted to know. I was surprised Johnny had only stirred a few times through all of this. "Wake up!" she said into his ear and rubbed his head.

"*Don't Jennifer!*" It was Melanie. "We have to be nice to him. He's just a baby."

"I want to see his eyes," said Jennifer.

"Newborns all have blue eyes," I said. "They also need lots and lots of sleep. He's not even a day old yet."

Then they were full of questions. Does he have a belly button? Does he stay with me all the time? Who gets to feed him? Did it hurt when he came out of my stomach? I answered all their questions, happily, untiringly, wishing the moment would last. It had been eight long months since we'd had a joyful moment such as this in our family. We'd been through such dreary times. But life had sprung anew for us and I felt a joy surpassed only by what I had felt in heaven. Baby Johnny was filling a vacant spot in the family. There were seven of us again.

I saw the joy in my children's beaming faces and started to cry.

"Are you okay?" Melanie asked.

"Yes," I answered. "I'm just happy."

"When are you and Johnny coming home?" she wondered. "It's almost Christmas."

"I know it is. We'll come home soon, honey. We'll have a wonderful Christmas together."

Shortly, it was time to go. After many hugs and kisses—for me and the baby—Grandpa and Grandma gathered the kids and took them home.

My heart glowed all the rest of the day. My children had blessed me by their innocence, their energy, and their love. I couldn't wait to get home. Things were going to be so different now.

The next couple of days in the hospital passed in a blur. I spent my time resting and reading all the cards and letters that came pouring in from friends and family. And I continued writing in my journal. Also, there was a stack of Christmas cards my mother had brought for me to read. It was wonderful to be remembered by so many.

Dr. Jackson was surprised at how quickly I was recovering. Though the effects of C-sections are usually slow to heal, I was experiencing less pain from the surgery and less sting from the stitches than I had when Clint was born. My energy was returning, and soon I was becoming restless.

By the end of the third day I was ready to go, and the insurance company agreed with me. But Dr. Jackson thought one more day of rest would do me good.

"Besides," he said, "I don't think you could drag that baby away from those nurses. He's a little charmer."

I laughed.

"I think everyone who was there has mentioned to me about the feeling in the room when he was born. Most of us are religious around here—we know what birth is all about. But some births are more memorable than others. This one was special, Chris."

"It was," I said. "It really was."

I hid a whole world behind my smile.

I did stay another day. And on the morning of the fifth day, I was up early getting packed. Christmas was in two days, and I was anxious to be with my children. Because of the surgery it had been decided that I would spend several days, including Christmas, at my parents' home. So, it was they who came to get Johnny and me. We said good-bye to the nurses and orderlies and everyone who had been so helpful and kind. Then we loaded everything in the car and headed for Holden.

But once we got to my parent's home and situated inside, a nagging feeling entered my heart. It grew worse as the day progressed. I was comforted being in my parents' home; Mom was helpful with the children and with little Johnny. But I couldn't shake the feeling that I wanted to be in my own house for Christmas. I had planned for it and even *fought* for it when my pregnancy had overstayed its welcome. I just felt I belonged *there* for the holiday instead of here. I explained my feelings to Mom and Dad and they understood, as I knew they would. They agreed to take me home the next day.

"But, don't overwork yourself, Chris," my dad said, "or you'll end up flat in bed."

"I'll take it easy," I assured them.

And so it was, that I arrived with my new baby and all my other children at my own house on the day of Christmas Eve. Snow lay all around the yard and on the eaves of the house. Christmas decorations adorned the windows. It was like a Christmas cottage, I thought, and when we drove into the driveway, my heart leapt with excitement to see it. Yes! This was right! We belonged *here.* This was our home. It wouldn't have been Christmas anywhere else. My most tender feelings were centered here, around my family, and around my husband, whose presence I had felt here many times since his death.

When I walked through the door carrying little Johnny I was greeted by the sight of our beautiful Christmas tree. Its fresh pine scent filled the house with an aroma that invoked fond memories and warm emotions of Christmases past. In the kitchen and sitting around the house were many handmade goodies and crafts that neighbors and friends had brought to share.

"This is your new home," I said softly to Johnny, who was sleeping soundly in my arms. I walked past the living room and down the hall to my bedroom. I went to the crib, which was filled with soft blankets and downy quilts, and laid him in it. Then I stood looking down at him with a mother's tender love. Having him here in my room was like having him in my heart. He was safe and secure and nearby where I could watch over him and give

him huge doses of all my best loving, whenever he—or I—
needed it.

I went out to see that the other children had gotten in
with all of their luggage. We waved good-bye to Grandpa
and Grandma and then everyone wanted to see baby
Johnny in his crib. So we all tip-toed down the hall and
into my room, and in a minute there were six wide-eyed
faces peering over and through crib bars at a slumbering
newborn. When we all had our fill, everyone tip-toed back
out again and into the living room. By the expression on
the children's faces, I could see already how the presence of
little Johnny was renewing the spirit of life in our home.

The afternoon wore into evening. The setting sun
cast a spectacular rosy light against the snow-covered
mountains. Christmas lights on the houses of our street
flickered to life, and soon the entire neighborhood was
aglow with Christmas cheer. Christmas Eve, that much
awaited night, had finally come to Holden. I knew all the
people in town were gathering in their homes to reenact
family traditions made sacred through years of devotion to
family and to God.

Soon it was time for the annual ward Christmas
party. Members of my family from both sides came to
wish me Merry Christmas and to help get the children
ready. My girls put on their new Christmas dresses and
Michael and Clint wore handsome matching sweaters. My
children looked like angels on their way to the church.

When they came home, we said good-bye to the rela-
tives, taking promises for visits the next day, when there
would be new toys to share, dinners to be eaten, and a

special Christmas Day party at the Monsen's. When the last family member left, we shut the door and prepared ourselves for our own special party.

We got our pajamas on, ate some goodies, and talked about the presents under the tree and how exciting it would be when morning came and we could open them.

Then I brought Johnny in and sat with him on the couch, and all the children gathered around. On a table nearby sat our nativity scene, glazed a shiny white, and glowing under the lights on the Christmas tree. I picked up its pieces one by one and told in simple language the story of Christmas—that shepherds abiding in a field heard angels sing, that wise men followed a star to Bethlehem Town, that when the Baby Jesus was born, his mother laid him in a manger of hay, a humble bed for the Savior of the World.

Then Clint, our now talkative two-year-old, said, "Mommy, we have Baby Jesus at our house."

All eyes turned to little Johnny.

"Well, not Baby Jesus," I said. "But we do have Baby Johnny. Our special baby."

Then Jennifer wanted to sing "Silent Night." And in our hearts, and in our home, all was calm, all was bright.

When the music ended, the phone rang. It was Santa Claus, calling to tell the children that they had better go to bed so he could come visit. They all talked to him and afterwards gathered excitedly in the living room where we had family prayer. Then they ran to their rooms and jumped into bed. I didn't hear a peep after that. Soon they were sound asleep.

I laid out the children's presents and then shut off the lights. Only the tiny bulbs on the tree illuminated the room. Then I drew Johnny into my arms and sat rocking him quietly while he slept. So much had transpired since I first knew he was growing inside my womb. So much had changed. And yet, I had my children. We had our home. We would go on, in spite of whatever came our way. Now that I knew there was glorious purpose behind all things, I would wait, even in darkest times, for light to dawn. In faith, I would *expect* it. For beyond our mortal view was a world of light and beauty enough for every darkened soul, peace and tranquility for every troubled mind, comfort for every tragedy, and love, magnificent, transcendent love, for every wounded heart. My husband was there in that place and would be waiting for my return. He had pointed the way to get there—it was through the Savior, Jesus Christ, who, if I laid all my trust in him, would guide me to eternity. He was my Solace, my Shepherd, my Friend.

The hour was late, but I continued to rock Johnny in my arms, letting the night grow full and rich around me. Love for my son swelled my heart, and I believe I felt for an instant what Mary might have felt for her Special Baby, holding him in her arms so long ago.

I looked at sweet Johnny snuggled close to my breast. *Sleep in heavenly peace,* I thought.

Epilogue

Today, more than seven years later, memories of my husband's drowning are still vivid. Every time I travel the interstate past the Yuba Lake turnoff, I shudder. I went back to the lake only once, to do research for my story. While there, I noticed some changes—the rickety dock where we boarded the boat has been replaced by two new, modern ones. The cement pad at the top of the ramp where I sat my children is grown over with shrubs. There are more access paths carved from the road to the lake. And most noticeably, drought conditions have caused the water level to drop significantly, rendering the old shoreline almost impossible to make out. I consider these changes good and would be happy if every reminder of that dread day were transformed or erased. Nevertheless, it is *still* Yuba Lake—the wind still blows, and the water is cold, rough, and murky. I hope never to return there again.

As for our boat, it sits covered by a tarp in a ramshackle shed surrounded by overgrown weeds. It is no one's favorite boat anymore.

However, these grim reminders of John's death do not make me afraid of dying. My visit with John vanquished that fear. When my time comes, I will welcome death. It is merely a door to my real home, a conveyance back to my husband's arms.

As for my children, each one has experienced the stages of grief, of questioning, of resentment, of struggling to accept life without their dad. I answer frankly when they ask about John's death; by a certain age, general details don't satisfy. But how he died is only half the story. The other half, *my half*, is the part that brings understanding. It blesses them with a legacy of comfort and hope that always tempers their sadness. And my children are seldom sad. Resiliency and courage more often define their response to hardship, which has been an example for me to learn from.

In our home, I have tried to follow the counsel John gave during my visit with him. I do this by making sure we pray together, read the scriptures, study the words of the prophets, and go to our meetings. But most importantly, in these seven years, I have sought to establish a home with Christ as its foundation. I have tried to lead my children to the Savior, to help them learn of him and know his ways. Being a single parent remains a challenge. But John's love for his children and his confidence in me inspires me to do my best. My knowledge of the spirit world blesses me with peace even when difficulties arise at home. With the Lord as my partner, I am finding a measure of success at parenting and joy along the way. We've been blessed with his Spirit in our home. And I've learned that the capacity of children to grasp spiritual things is remarkable. Growing up in an environment where their spirits may flourish, my children are emerging as highly unique and vibrant personalities, and from this mother's perspective, my kids are a marvel to see!

Johnny is six now. The older he gets, the more he reminds me of his father. He's still a charmer and is doted upon by everyone, especially his three sisters, who spoil him shamelessly. As he grows, a sense of recognition whispers that it was *his* spirit who came with John that morning to my room—when I was told not to rush things, that the baby needed time. I also believe it was Johnny who assisted his father in giving me a blessing when I was in the spirit world. To contemplate this fills me with wonder. One thing I'm sure of: Johnny and I have something in common. Though he has no conscious memory of it, we two have associated with John in the spirit world and know him as the wise and loving being of light he now is. Once in a while, my son's expression or gesture will so perfectly mimic his father's, that I know John put him up to it when they were together. These little echoes of John's wit catch me off guard, which I know must delight my husband.

In our family we have embraced Johnny as our living link to Dad. Sometime after he was born, I had Johnny's name added to his brother's and sister's names on John's headstone. I also had a photo of him superimposed over the family photo taken two days before John's death. In the composite photo, he sits in his father's lap, which was left vacant in the original, as if for this very purpose. It comforts us to see this representation of our complete family.

As our children grow older, raising them requires a lot of emotional energy. Getting away with friends for shopping or a game of softball helps me stay balanced. Regular sessions at the temple do the most to rejuvenate my spirits.

But I miss John terribly sometimes. Not because of despair or self-pity, but simply because I still need him. My zest for life has returned and even increased. But getting used to living without him does not mean getting to like it. Knowing where he is helps, but sometimes I cry because I know he's having a great time there without me. Having knowledge that life continues on the other side only makes it easier for me to believe I'm being "ignored" by the one I love when he doesn't check in. When I feel this way, I want to shout, "Don't you forget me, John Monsen!"

Sometimes I remember his bright, intelligent spirit, and I feel left behind and inferior. He's able to advance in knowledge and light so much further and faster than I. But then I remember something I've come to believe: because of the opposition we face here, what to us seem to be little victories are seen on the other side as strides of accomplishment. Maybe enduring to the end is like faith: a little bit takes us a long way.

So I try to endure. And when I miss John too much, or my love for him overfills my heart and needs letting out, I hug my kids. Or, I call Lorna, or I go to the Lord— who understands completely how I feel. Sometimes I content myself with simply sending love in John's direction.

The veil is often thick—for a purpose—but I believe love passes through.

Mostly, I live by faith—faith that the Lord will catch me when I fall, forgive me when I err, and love me when I hurt. I'm learning to trust him, especially that living without John is for my good.

My extended family has continued to help and support me. My children are blessed to have a wide circle of uncles and aunts, grandparents and cousins, who love them and include them in their lives as if they were their own. While every family member has sacrificed for us, none has sacrificed more than Kelly, my loving, capable brother who, over the years, has more than lived up to his commitment to care for us.

Just beyond Kelly's home, at the crest of a little hill on the eastern edge of town, there is a special place of tranquility and comfort. I make regular pilgrimages there. It is John's grave. The headstone, marking his resting place near the blue spruce, looks as new as the day it was placed there. Sometimes the children go with me, especially on John's birthday and on other special days. Occasionally, we go just to talk, to remember him . . . to keep him alive in our hearts. And sometimes we feel him there—more alive than just within our hearts.

John still watches over us, especially the children, and occasionally we hear from him.

One morning, some neighbor kids were teasing Melanie at the bus stop. They didn't understand how her dad could have drowned in a lake. Was he a bad swimmer? They asked. It hurt Melanie's feelings, and she started to cry. She got on the bus and sat away from the others, tears rolling down her cheeks. Then warmth filled her heart, and she could tell that her daddy was sitting next to her, right there on the bus. He told her that she would be okay, that he was watching over her, and not to be afraid or feel sad. Then she felt something brush against her cheek and wipe her tears away.

John loves his children. He expresses it himself in the letter I wrote for him the night baby Johnny was born. These are John's own inspired words:

My Dear Children,

I love you more than words can express. I want the very best for each of you. You are such special children and are capable of taking on great responsibilities. But you must do your part. There is an eternal plan. You must follow it. Only then will you find joy. Grow in the gospel. Make it foremost in your life.

My children, here are some guidelines I want you to follow. They will be your keys to happiness:

1. Make Jesus Christ your foundation. When you come to know your Brother and Savior, you will see how very special you are to him. It is important to let him walk with you during your journey in life. Seek the Savior's guidance in all things, and he will help you.

2. Make the Church your cornerstone. You do this by attending your meetings, holding family home evenings, and following the prophet's teachings.

3. Pray always. Communicate with your Heavenly Father sincerely and faithfully, and he will help you.

4. Study the scriptures, and improve your knowledge through reading good books. Seek earnestly to gain the skills you need to be successful in life.

5. Learn to give of yourselves in true service to others. Love everyone with a pure and Christlike love.

Children, when the time is right, seek out a worthy mate. Choosing an eternal companion is one of the most important decisions in life. Seek out the best for yourselves and be sealed in the temple of the Lord. Then, in your marriage, make the Savior your foundation and the Church your cornerstone, and you and your companion will build the greatest mansion of eternal joy you can ever imagine.

I love your mother deeply, my children. Because of her love for you and her testimony, she will raise you the way I would have you raised. I want you to listen to her. She knows what is best for you. Follow her counsel, and she will enlighten you and plant within your hearts the seed of eternal joy.

Most importantly, know that I love you. I had a chance to speak with all of you just before I died. Look back on those memories and grasp the understanding that I love you and want the best for you. Whenever you are faced with trials and unhappiness, remember the guidelines I have given you.

I love you all, and I am watching over you. Do not forget. I am preparing the way for you to receive your greatest expectations.

Love,

Dad

My dear reader, Jesus Christ stands at the door and knocks. If you let him into your life he will bless you with all things good. He lives, and he loves you. Seek him, and he will endow you with his Spirit, and you will be glorified and raised up with him at the last day. You have a home with him and with a loving Father in the heavens. It is a world more beautiful than I have described. Your departed loved ones are there. They are waiting for you and are doing a preparatory work for that day of gladness when Christ will come again. Develop faith, yes, even enough to move a mountain, and you will remain untouched in the desperate days ahead when evil overruns the earth. Keep your families near you and know that the Lord will triumph. Make him your foundation, and all will be well. He will guide *you* to eternity. I testify that these things are true.

With love,
Christine Tuttle Monsen

About the Author and Her Children

Christine Tuttle was born in Springville, Utah. She grew up on a dairy farm with a great love for animals, the outdoors, and sports. Chris married John Monsen on April 20, 1979, and they became the parents of six children. Chris lives in Holden, Utah, with her children and provides the following update:

Melanie is fourteen now. She is sensitive to issues of right and wrong and has an unshakable desire to live the gospel. She runs track—getting speed from me and endurance from her father—and still holds the middle-school record for the mile.

Stephanie is thirteen. She loves to read, has a keen mind, and an excellent memory. She loves sports and dancing and is a friend to everyone, especially to those in need of friends.

Eleven-year-old Jennifer is a doer. Anything I ask of her gets done. She enjoys anything domestic. But most of all, she loves playing with her brothers. There's no child in my family who has ripped out more pants climbing trees than Jennifer.

Michael, my ten-year-old, is talented with his hands. Like his dad, he is mechanically minded and can fix most anything. He is also very keen to the Spirit. He loves to read his scriptures, bear his testimony, and is anxious to serve a mission one day.

Clint lives for sports. You name it, he plays it and excels at it—especially for a kid who's only eight! Clint is always conscious of my feelings and reminds the others to respect their mom.

Johnny will be seven this Christmas. The older he gets, the more he reminds me of his father. His energy is boundless. He thrives when he's outdoors and is forever without his shoes.